MONEY QUOTIENT

BUILDING FINANCIAL INTELLIGENCE IN YOUR CHILDREN

RAYMOND GABRIEL

MONEY QUOTIENT – BUILDING FINANCIAL INTELLIGENCE
IN YOUR CHILDREN
RAYMOND GABRIEL

Copyright © RAYMOND GABRIEL, 2015
Hard Cover : ISBN 978-967-13408-1-3

Address of the Publisher:
Mr. Raymond Dinesh Gabriel
No 4 Jalan SS 22/10
Damansara Jaya
47400 Petaling Jaya, Selangor,
Malaysia
www.raymondgabriel.com
info@raymondgabriel.com

Executive Editor:
Stephanus Kok
Cover Art & Layout Design:
 Zizi Iryaspraha S
www.pagatana.com

Table of Content

Dedication and Acknowledgements

I would like to dedicate this book to my wife Esther who has stood by me through bad and good times, and my two children Mia and Nora who always light up my life whenever I am near them. They have had to sacrifice much so that others could be blessed with trainings and writings.

I would also like to thank Dr. Jonathan and Helen David for almost 13 years of continuous input. Both of you are now reaping the harvest of what you have sown. I also want to thank Rohan Marshall, my business partner at People Systems Consultancy, who has labored together with me for more than 10 years. Also Cyrus Gomez who stood by me all those difficult years, and who initiated the idea to write this book.

Lastly, I would like to thank my friend Stephanus Kok, without whose guidance and ideas, this book would not have come off as well as it has done.

Thank you all. Success is not a solo project and this success belongs to all of you and many others who have helped along the way.

Foreword
by the Author

Many years ago I started teaching adults financial management principles for personal finance. I decided to teach in a practical way, making finance and investment principles easy to learn and easy to apply, and experiential in its methodology.

I noticed something very important while teaching these thousands of adults. There was a recurring pattern. Most of the adults I was teaching wanted to be rich and successful and were hungry for knowledge, or what many call financial intelligence, but most were in a place where they had already made mistakes and many of them were in trouble and in huge debt.

Even more disturbing was the fact that most had made these mistakes when they were quite young and were now trying to find a way to reverse their situations at an older age. I had a revelation and made a startling discovery.

Most of our financial habits are formed at an early age. Bad habits are observed being modeled by parents and learned by children. Most children think of money as a renewable resource, not a perishable limited stream. This is mainly because they observe adult behavior that reinforces the patterns of spending money as a resource with unlimited supply. This is also why a lot of principles in this book are aimed at adults to practice and then model as positive behaviors or habits for their children. Children learn more by observing how we behave, rather than listening to what we say.

Children in the age to come are going to need different types of financial intelligence to function as adults in an increasingly expensive, competitive and changing world. IQ alone is not going to cut it. We are going to need a Money Quotient (MQ)! To adequately prepare them for the world to come we are required to equip them with these new types of financial intelligence or MQ.

Most of this book is designed on sound principles of managing finance and incorporates strategies to give you the tools to work these principles at two levels; with children 5-12 years of age and with adolescents 13-19 years of age.

It is never too late to learn. Who knows? By going chapter by chapter, and working out these principles with your child and taking your time to ensure they learn properly, you might set your child up to have an edge on his peers, his society, and his world in the future. I believe these are the tools your child will need not just to survive but to THRIVE in the age to come.

Be Blessed and Prosperous,

Raymond Gabriel

MONEY QUOTIENT

BUILDING FINANCIAL INTELLIGENCE IN YOUR CHILDREN

Introduction
to Money Quotient

Managing money is a key factor that determines success in life. I have seen many people who are highly educated and who hold high positions fail and crumble with their financial life because they did not practice or live the right financial principles.

I have also seen people who are not so highly educated and who do not have a good grasp of language or communication achieve great wealth because they practice the right wealth accumulation principles and have the right mindset and attitude towards money.

Academic Intelligence, or natural brilliance is not a key determining factor to success in life, but your financial intelligence is. I call this your financial quotient, or *Money Quotient* (MQ) as reflected in the title of this book.

Some people believe that the best way to gauge a person or

a child is to test their intelligence quotient or IQ. I, however, believe in the concept of multiple intelligences. Each child has a gift or an intelligence in a particular area.

At the Harvard School of Education a psychologist named Howard Gardner, while accepting the IQ test as a form of intelligence assessment, also argued that there are 'other intelligences' (I am using my own words here to paraphrase his research). I feel that book smarts, or academic results are no longer adequate to prepare children to face the realities of life in this complex world of ours. We need to think about developing other intelligences in our children to get them ahead in life.

I also believe, in terms of these multiple intelligences, that we do not have to accept that our child is only gifted in some areas and not so in others. I personally believe that any of the key intelligences that a child needs can be developed. Music is an example. Some experts say that the ability to sing in tune and appreciate music is not something that a child is born with, but it is developed through exposure to music at a young age. Imagine if we start developing our children in other intelligences besides academics at an early age?

I think there are no limits to the various core intelligences that can be developed in a child. I also believe that more core intelligences than those I mentioned above can be developed in a child to enable them to achieve greater success in life. For example, for years one of the most underrated intelligences has been social intelligence, your ability to build trust, rapport and relationships with people easily. However, successful people know how to work with others, including difficult people.

One of the Most Important Intelligences

Of all the intelligences I think one of the core foundations to build for your child is their financial intelligence or Money Quotient. After all, it is a big part of whether your child will become a successful person in life (as you will read later in this book, I cite examples of average people with average incomes who become multi-millionaires), but more importantly, your child spends a big part of their lives studying to get into a good university. Once into university then they study some more to get good grades so that they can eventually get a good job or start a great business to become wealthy. If a huge part of their time is going to be spent in the pursuit of money, don't you think we should teach them financial intelligence? Shouldn't we develop their Money Quotient?

Throughout this book concepts that teach the acquisition, management, and multiplication of wealth will all be covered.

The Money Quotient or financial intelligence must be a foundation we give our children to succeed. Robert Kiyosaki, a well-known personal finance guru, wrote on why A grade students often work for C grade students. He articulated that book smarts do not necessarily equate to money smarts. I believe there is a significant difference. Academic success is no guarantee of success in life, but a high Money Quotient or strong financial intelligence will give our children an edge over their peers.

How to Use This Book

This book is written to help parents and children work a blueprint to thrive with their finances. There are two ways to read this book.

Firstly, you can read this book as a reference manual and select the chapters you feel are most relevant and go straight for those chapters. You could then return to eventually work your way through the other chapters.

Secondly, you can read this book cover to cover, as a course book, systematically working your way through the lessons and exercises to thoroughly assimilate the information presented.

I recommend the second way of going through the book for the reasons outlined below:

- All chapters in this book follow a flow of learning. If you jump a chapter you might miss an element of importance you need to develop in yourself or your children that will be of immense benefit to you.

- While certain elements such as investment or budgeting might look more appealing to us to teach our children, getting our children to have the right mindsets before content and knowledge is transferred is even more important.

- The mindset alignment chapters are the first two chapters of this book and these chapters are critical. A foundation needs to be laid in the mind and spirit of the child before knowledge is given and transferred. Without this foundation, knowledge can become theoretical instead of practiced, and well taught principles.

- Working through management of money is important to do before you move into growing your wealth through investment. If principles are not properly laid to handle money, you can easily make big mistakes with investment and lose all you have gained.

- Think of this book as a holistic, step by step process to lay a foundation with your children that they will remember for life. It is important that areas are not skipped and overlooked because everything has a link to an overall process of development in the mind, spirit and body.

A Summary of the Chapters and Flow of This Book

Listed below is a summary and flow of the content so that you can understand how I have written this book and why I have written it in this way.

Chapters One and Two, *'Principle of Delayed Gratification'* and *'Emotions and Money'* deal with mindsets and attitudes towards money. I have found from the many adults I have counseled that their main financial problems stem from the wrong attitudes and mindsets that they have towards money, not their lack of skills and intelligence in financial matters. Many people know the right thing to do, but still cannot empower themselves to do it. The reason for this is if your attitudes and mindsets do not change, it is impossible to practice and develop new behaviors and actions. Starting with the foundation of cultivating the right mindsets and attitudes is a critical first step before you learn techniques and tactics.

Chapters Three and Four, *'Wealth for a Cause'* and *'Wealth Acquisition Principles'*, deal with what I like to call 'Laws of attraction of wealth'. When these concepts are practiced you set yourself up to attract opportunities, people and favor. Attracting wealth can be structured and developed. It is a powerful concept that can keep you and your children resourced for life. Chapter Four lays out the Principles of Wealth, which when practiced, can stop you from losing hard earned money. "It is easier to spend a dollar and harder to earn it," my mentor always used to say. The principles I share in this chapter, if practiced, will help us to retain wealth. Wealth for a cause, in chapter three teaches how a cause can bring supernatural increase and can take the little you have to greater heights. I have seen this happen in my own life and I have tried to structure this as a blueprint for you to work through to develop your own cause in life.

Chapters Five and Six, *'Setting a Budget'* and *'Expense Tracking'*, are chapters that focus on how you can manage your money to stay on track with your financial goals. Many people have lofty goals with no way of achieving them. One of the most important things that we need to do is to set an achievable, realistic budget that is geared towards our goals. Chapter six teaches how we can align our lives, expenses and emotions to stay on track with the budget so that we can achieve the goals we set. I have met many people who want to invest in land, properties and shares but do not have the basic capital to do so. The reason is because they are not living according to their financial plan and adjusting their lifestyle daily to achieve the capital needed to start investing in things that can bring them huge returns to achieve even bigger goals. These chapters also include simple tools and strategies you can practice, without adding much stress, to get started and stay committed towards your financial plan.

Chapter Seven, *'Investment 101'*, covers the basic rules of investment and teaches concepts and principles you must follow if you want to be successful with investments and in growing your wealth. It also teaches practical do's and don't and deals with fundamental investment best practices. Don't have a hearing mentality and get into investments just because your friends and family are doing it. Get into investing for the right reasons and choose the right investments that fit your own risk profile. This chapter even has a risk profiling process where you can test yourself and your children, and use it to align your investments too. There are also certain types of investments which you must avoid as they are nothing more than scams. This chapter teaches you how to tell the difference between a legitimate investment and a scam.

Chapter Eight, *'Debt Management'*, is a very interesting topic that most of my friends seem to be very interested in. Many of us have debt and sometimes some of us can be in a bad financial situation pressured by huge debts. This chapter teaches the difference between good debt (credit facilities) and bad debt, how to use debt to grow our financial muscle, and also how to get out of debt and its pressure if you are facing it. Debt is a useful tool if you know how to use it, but don't fall for the common traps people get into and cannot get out of, that are outlined in this chapter. We always hear "prevention is better than a cure" for a disease. Debt, if not managed properly and structured well, can be like a bad disease.

Chapter Nine, *'Working the Economic Cycles'*, is a chapter that focuses on the economic cycles every country or trading block goes through. It teaches how you can prepare for and thrive in a recession. Recession time is opportunity time for those who are set up well. Having cash is just one of the ways you can set yourself up well. Your research and planning for opportunities that will be opened during bad economic periods is vital as well. This chapter talks about how to set yourself up during economic boom periods to capitalize during recession periods. It also gives tips to survive during catastrophic depression or collapses of whole financial systems.

Chapter Ten, *'Winning at Business Early'*, teaches how we can work with our children from a young age to get them to start their own business. It is a guide to get a business project going with each of your children. Business is a foundation you can give your children so that they do not become trapped in a system of working for others as a means of livelihood and survival. You can prepare your children to beat the system and thrive in this world. This chapter gives very practical concepts and methodologies on how you can start, what you can do, and how to do it.

As I have mentioned previously, all the chapters flow with and build upon one another, and I have tried to be as concise and complete as I can. You won't find everything in this book, however this book will address certain gaps in financial knowledge which are not covered by other books, and it can give you a good start on your journey towards developing your MQ (Money Quotient).

Chap 1 &2	Chap 3&4	Chap 5&6	Chap 7	Chap 8	Chap 9	Chap 10
Mindsets and Emotions to Grow Wealth	Laws of Attraction to Attract Wealth	Management of Wealth	Growing Your Wealth via Investment	Debt Management Traps to Avoid	Economic Cycles Thriving on Recession	Starting Business Early Get an Edge

After every chapter, I have written some practical steps and exercises we can do and enjoy with our children to practically work out the concepts. The exercises are age specific, some are simple for younger age groups and some are more complex for older children and youth that need a detailed grasp of the concepts explained.

My hope is that you will enjoy this book, enjoy the process and that the concepts in this book will expand your boundaries according to the potential you already have inside you, and allow you to expand the boundaries of your children according to the unlimited potential they embody within.

Chapter 1

Delayed Gratification

The Cornerstone of a Strong Financial Foundation

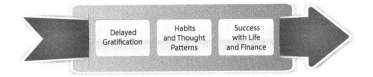

Results of Practicing Delayed Gratification

How can practicing the concept of delayed gratification build superior character in your child that will set them up for financial success? It can do so in a number of ways including, most notably, the following:

1. Strong Work Ethic

Work ethic isn't just working hard by putting in the hours. It is working hard to get the right results for the situation. Work ethic means you have to work consistently harder than others and pay the price while others sometimes take the easy way out. Guess what? Everyone who has work ethic almost always succeeds. It's one of the foundations for success. How do you get your child to do her homework first and play later? Basically by cultivating a great work ethic. To do this they need to master the concept of delayed gratification. Work ethic will set our children up for a life of success in work, business, finances and investment, and many other areas of life.

2. Emotional Control

We are going to cover this in more detail in chapter two, but most impulse buying is linked to a lack of control over emotions. Delayed gratification teaches a child how to delay or not give in to these impulses, thereby allowing the child to save more, in turn giving the child more investment capital, which allows the child to invest more and become rich faster.

3. Sacrifice

In his best-selling book, 'The Outliers', Malcolm Gladwell talks about the "rule of 10 000", which basically states that if you want to be a genius or great at something you have to do it for 10 000 hours. He cites the Beatles who did this by playing in front of crowds in Germany almost 10 hours a day, every day for a few years. Bill Gates did programming for several years when still a child through his school computer club.

I have watched Michael Jackson through interviews talk about how his father made him practice dancing for several hours a day from the time he was five years old while other children went out to play. Behind every gifted person's "gift" is probably years of practice – 10 000 hours. It is a sacrifice, but delayed gratification is the key to get your child to want to pay the price for success.

4. Drive

If you were to ask me what is one of the most fundamental keys of success? I would tell you that it is drive. The ability to push through, pay the price and get something done, or to build something at all costs, that drive is the difference between those who succeed and those who do not. It is a critical key success factor. When things go wrong, and believe me they will, our children will feel like giving up, taking it easy and doing less. The concept of delayed gratification builds in your child the ability to drive and achieve a goal by working harder now with little immediate reward to enjoy the full benefits of it later.

Picture a scenario where a three year old is screaming loudly because he wants to eat something other than what is bought for him. The mother who is with the little boy first tells him to just do it. That fails, then she tries to distract him, this also does not work, so she then gets angry and shouts and threatens the child, and not surprisingly this fails as well. Finally, exasperated and embarrassed for the scene the child has created, she gives in to him by giving him what he wants and sighs "Humph. Why are you so difficult? You make me so angry!"

If the mother continues doing this with a child, then every time the child wants his own way in something, enforcing this negative habit will cause major problems within the child.

It may look like we have solved the problem in the now, because the child does not shout and scream any more, but in reality we have just sabotaged the principle of delayed gratification. Delayed Gratification is an important principle, not just with money but in all areas of life.

Now picture a teenager screaming and shouting because she does not want to do her homework, but she wants to go out partying with her friends who are bad company and not good role models. She wants to enjoy what she wants now instead of seeing how living for the future will help her more. So just to pacify her, the father says, "Finish your homework, then you can go." He has just sabotaged his child's future.

If we eat whatever we want, whenever we want, we will

become overweight and unhealthy very quickly because we are not delaying our gratification. However, if eating sugary foods is a special treat for which we delay the gratification to once in a while, we teach and discipline our body to delay the gratification for a greater ongoing and future benefit – which is better health.

The principle of delayed gratification applies in all aspects of life including marriage, work, good habits, learning, and other important relationships. Imagine a friend who wants to do what he wants, when he wants, regardless of other people. He certainly would not have many friends for long.

Simply put, those who do not practice this principle of delayed gratification do not succeed in life. Those who do, have a distinct edge over others, because many people have not had the awareness in life to live by this principle.

Delayed gratification also applies to money in a big way. One major observation I have made as I train people is that while many people want quick approaches to make millions and invest in good assets like property, most of them cannot even raise the capital to make these investments. They are literally capital-less. Even if I tell them of a sure-fire opportunity with guaranteed returns, they have no investment capital whatsoever with which to take advantage of such an opportunity. They have never delayed spending in the moment, in return for the greater benefit of accumulating capital for the future.

Applying Delayed Gratification

Where can delayed gratification be applied?

1. In Fields of Study

They will study first then enjoy the benefits after they finish gaining what they need.

2. At Work

They will excel as employees who finish what they start and pay the price to get things done on time. This is a rare commodity in the job market these days and will be even more so in the future to come.

3. With Health

They will exercise first and pay the price to be healthy because they can resist the urge to loaf around and just vegetate in front of the TV.

4. With Eating Habits

They will eat what they need to because they know it's good for their body in the long term.

5. With Money

They will save money first because they know not to give in to impulses.

6. With Business

They will work harder than employees, or others because they know they are investing in and for their future.

7. With Purchases

They will delay buying the latest and greatest to save money for investments that will grow their cash.

No Financial Growth Without Investment Capital

If you do not have investment capital you cannot take advantage of any opportunities for financial growth.

Why do people suffer from this malady? They want to learn, they want to invest in the right things, but they don't have enough money. Why?

Because they do not have the right financial habits, they live from month to month and paycheck to paycheck. For you to become an investor you must first be able to save. For you to save you must have the right habits, for you to have the right habits you must understand the concept of delayed gratification.

If our children can understand the concept of delayed gratification with money and practice this principle, it will give them a great edge in life. We will have cultivated in them crucial habits, like saving, that will inevitably result in them being successful in accumulating capital. They will then have enough capital to make investments and take advantage of opportunities from which they will reap the rewards way into their future.

Our children will have the edge because they avoid being like more than 90% of the world's population, some of whom are very well educated academically. Everybody wants to have more wealth, invest their money and multiply their money, but they do not practice the delayed gratification it takes to have the capital to even start.

Building the Habit of Delayed Gratification

How does one build the habit of delayed gratification into your child? To answer this you have to ask another question first. What makes people want to spend money to keep buying new things even when they do not need them? The answer is our perception of reward and the need to get our desires satisfied immediately.

Here is what you could do to build the concept of delayed gratification into your child:

1. Say No Regularly

Say no to your child when your child wants to buy something and if it is really not necessary to buy an item. Do this on a regular basis. The child will learn "I cannot always get what I want, when I want" and this allows the child to find other outlets for himself. However, be very careful not to deprive your child though. If our child is seriously deprived they will build resentment towards being tightfisted and then splurge when they become working adults with money. Find appropriate times to say yes and no.

2. Create Opportunities to Reward Excellence

Create jobs in the household for your children to do and get them to do it with excellence for them to gain rewards. Come up with a rating system, inspect their work with a monthly sheet and give them a rating. For example _ Cleaning the table after dinner; get your child to clean the table and rate it from one to five. If he does it excellently, give him a score of five, if badly a score of one. Develop a one page sheet for you to tick every day. The average they get determines different reward levels.

Firstly, the child will learn that nothing is for free and that they have to earn rewards. Secondly, they will raise the standard of what they are doing and be able to apply excellence in every other task given to them. It will create a pattern of excellence. You can still give them rewards on birthdays or if they achieve something extraordinary.

3. Demonstrate the Savings Potential of Waiting

Demonstrate, teach and instill in your child that if they wait before buying things, they can get it cheaper. Teach them to wait for sales and for new items to become old stock. Then show them by taking them to the stores and letting them see with their own eyes how things have gotten cheaper during the period of waiting. You just have to track the price of the item with your child.

For example, when the latest iPad or phone comes out, you know your teenager is going to ask you for one. All his friends have one and now he thinks he "needs" one as well. You will probably hear how his old one is not so great anymore and how it cannot do this or that. Let him know that you are going to wait for the price to come down. Take him to the store, record the price, then take him back to the same store after a period of time (about 3-6 months later) and show him the price again. Teach the child how to shop.

4.   Demonstrate and Cultivate the Habit of Saving Money

Make Saving Money a Game. Saving money whenever you can is a habit and it is easy to learn a new habit if you make it into a game. When I first got married I realized my wife had better habits than I did. She would switch off the lights when I left them on and left a room, she would switch off the air-conditioning when others left it on in the office and moved to another room. She would only buy during sale periods. She had a host of habits that would save us tons of money and get the family good deals.

She was winning the game by beating the system. We got holidays cheaper, and flights cheaper. We bought stationary for our business at the best rates. Everywhere she could negotiate or win us a better deal she would. When we analyzed her habits, most of the time we would realize that what she was doing was WAITING and SHOPPING AROUND for the better deal. It was delayed gratification in action.

Although at the time of writing this book my children are very young (3 and 5 ½ years old), they are constantly being exposed to her habits and now after having hers rub off on me, my habits have changed as well. Children need examples of the values we are preaching. They need to watch us practicing it so that they know we are serious about it and feel that it is important enough for us to implement in our own life. Don't be parents who preach what they don't practice.

Greed Covetousness and the Spirit of Poverty

Greed
- Wanting riches immediatly
- Wanting more without a purpose
- Brings unhappiness and financial ruin

Covetousness
- Wanting what others have all the time
- Causes us to rush out to buy with money we don't have to keep up with the Jones's
- Causes us to make bad financial decisions and delays the acquisition of wealth

A spirit of Poverty
- Causes us to fear money and the lack of it
- Causes us to make impulsive financial decisions, which can lead to financial ruin because of fear of lack
- Doesn't allow us to see thepossibilities of our life and future

There are three exceedingly bad habits that can come from a lack of delayed gratification. These three habits can come in, in a strong way and will undermine your child's financial success if your child does not have, or does not practice, delayed gratification.

EXERCISE: Delayed Gratification
Cornerstone of a Strong Financial Foundation

For Ages 5-12

The next time your child asks you for a toy, take him or her to a toy store. Tell them that they can have the toy provided they save and give you a percentage of their money every week.

You need to give them pocket money and teach them how to manage it. Once a week take them to a candy store or ice cream shop. Show them the ice cream, then tell them they can use the money they have saved to buy an ice cream for themselves or to keep saving it to buy the toy.

Keep showing them the toy once a month, or buy the toy and keep it in the house and let them see it once a week as well.

The money must be kept in a clear glass or plastic jar. Once a week get them to count the money and tell them how close they are, if they are young help them and teach them to count.

The object of this exercise is to build delayed gratification in a way they can understand gauge their progress.

If they can stop immediate gratification, they can live the reward of delayed gratification.

For Ages 13-17

Make a deal with your adolescent child the next time he asks you for a phone or for the latest tablet or some new gadget that all his friends have. Point him to the top of the line model that is better and tell him if he is willing to wait and work (A small business, chores with you, other youths, neighbors or in the community) to raise half the money for the top of the line model you will give him the other half.

Keep the deal and buy it for him, but go back to the store when the item is outdated about six to twelve months later and show him how much effort and money he could have saved if he just was willing to WAIT.

Explain delayed gratification to him in terms of money and teach him that this could make him rich.

Chapter 2

Emotions and Money
Setting the Right Emotions for Financial Breakthrough

Many of us have subtly picked up from various advertisements and media that we need to shop to release stress and reward ourselves. Many times just going out for a night at an expensive restaurant, going on a luxurious vacation, or other forms of spending releases become expenditures that we allow ourselves as rewards. The "need" for such *emotional pick-me-ups* is part of the culture of consumerism actively being propagated by the marketing media.

The message that we have subtly picked up is that it's okay to treat or reward yourself in ways you really cannot afford if your emotions are down.

What this does is link money spending to emotions. Most advertising messages subtly play on this link. In their study entitled *Consumer Kids - the Commercialization of Childhood,* Adriana Barbaro and Jeremy Earp talk about a cradle-to-grave marketing strategy that is being used by some advertisers to hook children on products.

Here are some key points taken from their study:

Key Points

- Children now spend $40 billion dollars of their own money and *influence* another $700 billion in spending annually – roughly the equivalent of the combined economies of the world's 115 poorest countries.

- Corporate marketers have studied the shopping behavior of kids, including the so-called *"nag factor,"* to help maximize the number of times children ask their parents for a product.

- Children are now marketed to in unprecedented ways – through brand licensing, product placement, viral marketing, via schools, DVDs, video games, the internet, cell phones – so that there's a brand in front of a child's face virtually every moment of every day.

- Because kids are now multi-tasking with media – simultaneously surfing the web, watching television, listening to their iPods, etc. – they are bombarded with over 3,000 commercial messages every day.

- In what the industry calls a *"cradle-to-grave"* strategy, marketers want to get to children early, often, and in as many places as they can – not just to sell them products and services, but to turn them into life-long consumers.

You can see this very clearly in McDonalds advertising campaigns that seek to get children hooked on fast food, knowing once they're hooked, they will crave it for life.

This is a global phenomenon. How does this affect my child with respect to emotional spending, you say? Well, every message that is targeted at children is playing with their emotions and telling them it is okay to spend money on products to feel better. In fact some messages say it is the only way to feel better.

Marketing Strategies to Note

These are some key areas and marketing strategies that you should look out for that you might not be aware of:

1. Product Placement

Product Placement is the most subtle form of advertising. Coke, for example, pays movie producers to place their product in movies. Audi paid for their cars to be featured in *The Transporter* movies - a cool way via movies that attracts a certain genre. With product placement, more often than not, the product is placed in a way that gives the actor emotional relief, or in the case of *The Transporter* movies, to make the lead actor look cool.

2. Endorsements

Chilldren always look up to their idols, and when their idols use a certain brand or endorse it, that subtlety plays in their minds that it is a good product.

3. Peer Influence

Older chilldren are susceptible to other children who have given in to their emotions and who feel emotionally elated for owning or buying a certain product. We have to protect our chilldren from this "latest is greatest" madness. Peer influence to buy the latest product is basically covetousness magnified. Advertisers influence chilldren with a subtle narrative that they are not emotionally complete as a person until they own or are seen with a certain item. Build integrity and a self-worth into your children that comes from who they are and not what they have. We have to model these things for our children to get the message across. If we are brand conscious and not quality conscious, we are sending the wrong message to our children.

My five year old daughter recently asked us to buy a certain product. When we asked her why that particular brand, She said, *"But it was on TV so it must be good."*

We realized that it is never too early to educate our children. We sat down and explained advertising and what marketing people were trying to do. Listed below are the key points of our message to our five year old. It was made easier because we had already explained basic business and customer concepts and have gotten her to start her first business at age five plus (I will talk about this a bit more in chapter 10).

- There is a game being played on television
- People are trying to make you use your money and your money to buy things by telling us it is good
- Not everything they say is good is really good. Sometimes they lie to you to sell you things
- You see that emotion of happiness the child had, she is acting, like how you act in your school playWhen you act is it real? Advertisements are not real either
- To win this game you have to ask and question whether what they are saying is true or not. You need to find out. You can ask daddy and mommy or you can learn from watching people who have bought what they are asking you to buy. Then you can choose whether you want to buy it or not

Advertisers use everything from sounds, visuals, and music to reach our sub conscious mind and emotions in order to sell their products as a feel good factor. This is the problem that causes us to link emotions to spending money, we do not do it consciously, however, it is our subconscious that has a direct influence on our behaviors.

Guarding Against the Advertising Onslaught

How do you protect your children and their emotions from the constant bombardment of advertising they are to face?

1. Recognize the Subconscious Message

Get your children to recognize that there are subconscious messages in advertising and product placements that are trying to trigger a response in them. Once they recognize it, they can subconsciously file what is being propagated as an untruth and will not recall it and subconsciously link it to an emotional spending behavior.

2. Choose Right to Win

Tell them it's a game; they win if they make informed choices about what they are being shown. Don't let them go for the first brand they see or the first product they want to buy. Teach them to compare, study value and make the best decision for products that they need based on a value/quality scale.

3. Do Not Rewards the Triggered Response

Ignore unnecessary nagging and desires from your child to buy and get things they want as a result of advertising. Your children will keep asking you to buy them stuff they see.

Usually it could start with *'my friend just got a new iPad, can I get the latest one too?'* Or if they are younger they will ask you to get that toy they just saw or buy an ice cream when passing by an ice cream store. These are basically emotional promptings. It is very important that you do not give in to them and reward the "programmed response" that is being triggered in them.

4. Overcome the Message

Explain to them they lose if they give in to a message, but win if they do not let it affect them. This brings us back to delayed gratification, the principle we talked about in the earlier chapter. Delayed Gratification can be built into our children at a very young age.

Habits Form Us If We Don't Form Habits

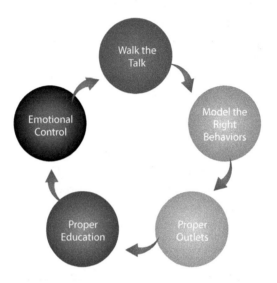

We have all heard this saying before, but I would like to show you some key areas in this saying, which might shed some light into financial education for your children.

1. Proper Outlet

Everybody including children go through stressful periods, it could be in a moment of time or it could be every day. Children face stress even in school, among peers and with schoolwork or teachers which are helping them with weak areas. Habits are formed as to how we handle stress or distress from a very early age. Some people eat sweet food to destress so their outlet becomes food, now you can see this in their weight. Some de-stress by watching television – where they sit and vegetate (thereby losing the potential of a stimulated mind), some shop and spend money, others go out for drinks, which can at times turn into an addiction. There are other addictions and cravings and bad habits.

The key is to build the right habits in our child as outlets for stress, enjoyment or relaxation from the start. For example taking a child to a playground instead of allowing them to vegetate in front of the TV tells them that enjoying the outdoors and physical activity is fun, exciting and a great free outlet (it is also a much more effective physiological release for stress and tension).

Another good outlet is getting them to talk to us about their day (and it is critical that we listen without judgment so they will share with us and talk to us freely). Let this become a habit in your child, as they learn to communicate and express in the right way, and to de-stress instead of keeping it all in and choosing bad outlets.

Enjoy a fun activity with your children every day so it can become a point of relationship building and a de-stressing activity for each child. The most important thing is for us to enjoy our children and to talk to them; encourage them to share their feelings as an outlet. Before we give them advice and correct their statements and feelings, it is vital to remember to validate what they are saying and put suggestions to them as a question. For example, "What do you think about looking at maths as a game or a puzzle instead of something that is heavy and unpleasant? Can it be done?"

Building proper outlets for our children teaches them to use their money well. They begin to learn control and what are proper outlets for their emotions. They become less likely to splurge or waste money on de-stressing while shopping. Teaching our children to have the right outlets in their life and how to use them at an early age will enable them to create proper outlets for themselves as they grow and as they need them.

2. Patience

Patience is not only a great habit but a virtue. I sometimes put treats like a cupcake or another goodie that my children like in front of them and get them to finish a task or their meal first. They can see what they like right in front of them. At first it is unbearable, then it gets easier and easier. We must honor our word to them. If we say, for example, we will give it to them if they finish their vegetables, then we must honor our word and give it to them when they have finished their vegetables. Never say to them, *"Okay, now I want you to also finish all the chicken on the plate."* Patience can be built when we earn their trust.

When it comes to spending money, we have to see how patience plays a big part in their financial lifestyle and habits. There was a young boy in a financial intelligence class we used to run who came from a wealthy family. Every three months or so, when the latest model mobile phone would be released, he would pressure his parents to buy him one and dispose of or sell off his old phone at a cheaper price.

He had a friend who would always buy these phones from him. The friend was a classmate, also from a wealthy background, but he kept buying second hand phones from him at a much cheaper price. After attending our financial intelligence class and learning about delayed gratification, this boy had a revelation. He said, *"My friend is benefiting from my impatience, if I just wait three to six months, I can get exactly what I want for a lot less"*. So he joined his friend in waiting and bought cheaper second hand phones from their other friends who were also wealthy. Great things come to us at a much lower cost, if we have patience and are willing to delay our gratification for the latest and greatest. Teach your child the right spending habits. Buy quality, not cheap brands (buying the cheapest is not always the best use of money as cheap seldom lasts. Buy quality on sale instead). The habit of patience is one habit that must be strongly built into our children.

3. Use Routine to Enable Good Habits

Establish good habits as routine in the life of your child so that they will automatically avoid the bad habits. Exercise, diet, and saving money are all great habits. If we start young and are consistent with them, they do not leave space for bad habits to form in those areas. Life does not exist in a vacuum. If we don't set good habits, something else will fill the space. Most of the time the space is filled with bad habits. For example saving as a habit is something we must do with our children every day. Give each child pocket money every day and get your child to decide as soon as they get it how much they want to save. Give them a clear see through jar, so that they can see the amounts accumulating and increasing. This becomes a visual motivator for them to save more. Keep affirming and encouraging this behavior as well so that your child learns that he earns your approval as a parent if he practices this good habit. The habit being formed here is the decision making of how much to save when receiving money (pocket money, salary or income). After the decision is made he can determine and adjust his lifestyle and manage his expenses with what he has left.

Now we must also temper this with a reward, for example getting our child to use part of the money for something they would enjoy. A trip if the child is older, or an item they always wanted to purchase. The key to forming good habits is that they must see and enjoy the rewards of forming the habit.

Eating healthy and on time is another example. Most of the time our children eat fast food because their eating habits are not planned for accurately, and we are the culprit for this. Taste buds and preferences are formed. If our child keeps eating healthily at home, they will have taste buds that dislike sweet, fried and salty foods. They will naturally avoid too much of such foods when out.

If our kitchen is another fast food chain outlet, guess what their taste-buds are going to be like? Bad eating habits can cause a child to waste a lot of money on eating out. It is unhealthy, which in turn will cause a child to pay excessive medical bills when they are older on health related problems.

Another key area is time management. Most of the time children vegetate in front of the TV, or surfing the web or Face booking with friends instead of using their time wisely to grow a small business, or learn something new, or even an exercise activity (a habit that can save their life in the future).

Imagine if your child uses his time to create and run a small business using Facebook instead of just hanging out with his friends doing something unproductive? Your child will enjoy it whilst learning that time can be used to grow wealth, instead of wasting it, and develop their potential.

Think of every area in your child's life that needs the right habits formed: diet, exercise, emotional control and outlets, and time management. Give due diligence to form the right habits or the wrong alternatives will naturally form in your child.

This is a key area in financial management because we have to think and plan what habits we want to work out with our children and plan for these early in a structured way. Good financial habits negate the inculcation of bad ones.

4. Walk the Talk

As parents we need to model the right outlets, expressions and habits. Habits will only work with our children if our children see us practicing them and behaving in the same way that we are asking them to behave. They need us to walk the talk. How many of us had parents say, *"You need to save, savings are important."* If they kept telling us this, why didn't we practice it? Probably because they never practiced this and thereby demonstrated to us how this was important.

Another aspect of this is including our children in our financial decisions, those that are not stressful, so that they learn how we are planning our resources and saving and investing. Get them involved in your discussions and sharing on finance. One of the best places and times to do this is around the table at dinner time. The Kennedy's used dinner time at home, not to talk about silly things, but to discuss politics. This made their children politically aware and each of the Kennedy children went on to become key figures in politics. Talk about savings and investment is not just for adults. It allows children to understand that it is an area of importance that needs to be given time and thought to.If we tell our children that informed decisions are important and that they should not buy on impulse, then we cannot go to a shopping centre and buy on impulse either.

We have to analyze our life on a regular basis and see what is not being modeled well.

- Is it the way we communicate?
- Is there enough exercise in our life and do we have healthy eating habits?
- Is there the practice of the right financial principles, or the opposite?

Analyze the various areas in your life regularly. Talk to your spouse and work through difficult areas so that your children see a model who walks the talk. Pay particular attention to the way you manage money, how you spend it and the amount of time you take to talk about savings and investments in front of your children.

Before my wife and I got married we talked about our habits that we felt needed to change so that we could model it when the children came along. We started eating right, we started different savings accounts to manage our money better, and we started tracking all our expenses. We even started communicating and modeling right behaviors with each other. All this was done before we had any children so that when the children came there would be nothing major to change in our behavior.

Start building habits into your children when they are young, don't wait until it's too late.

Avoiding the Emotional Spending Habit

How do you avoid emotional spending becoming a habit in your children?

Here are some things you can do:

1. Enjoy Low-Cost or Free Activities

Teach your children to enjoy activities, which are low-cost or free. We need to show them that not every activity we engage in is necessarily linked with spending money. In today's urbanized city environment, children learn that unwinding and relaxing means walking in malls and being subject to tons of messages and merchandise. This builds a culture of emotional spending in your child. One of the most wonderful things you can do with your child is to enjoy the outdoors. Gardening, hiking, parks, and other places where nature can be enjoyed are places that you can go to with your child. They will see a pattern of you having proper outlets for your emotions and will pick up this habit from you.

2. Optimizing the Use of Time

Teach your child to use time well. Most of us never learnt how to use and manage our time well. Time is one of the key resources that can be used to generate, manage and multiply money. In the book, 'The Millionaire Next Door', the authors Thomas J. Stanley and William D. Danko share the results of a study on habits that millionaires practice and reported that millionaires spend a lot of their time (approximately 8 hours a month) planning and organizing their finances. They also track every dollar. For a simple tracking tool that auto-calculates your expenses, visit my website www.raymondgabriel.com

3. Second-Hand Goods

Get your children used to the idea of using second-hand goods in good condition. The current generation is a generation of cavemen that need everything new and shiny. Why not get better value by buying high quality used and second-hand items that are in great condition. You do not have to spend top dollar for something new, but can profit off other's expenditure instead.

4. Talking About Emotional Difficulties

Teach your children how to talk their way out of emotional difficulties rather than engaging in the wrong outlets. Earlier we discussed how people go shopping to de-stress or they go clubbing, spend money on lavish lifestyles, and impulse buy to help cope with life and their emotions.

Addictions to alcohol, drugs and many other negative habits are the result of wrong outlets for emotional issues.

Many people around the world spend lots of money on therapists and   psychologists to talk about emotions. Why not be that for your own children? Get them to talk to you, build trust with them, allow them room to speak to you without judging them, and then give advice when asked (unless something is serious enough that you need to step in straight away). Set up friends around them who have the same values and can influence them in a positive way. These pre-emptive steps allow you to avoid dangerous and unproductive outlets in your child's life.

5. NO Tantrums Allowed

DO NOT tolerate tantrums... in both younger and older children. It is very important that we do not tolerate whining or tantrums. Always encourage your children to express themselves well and to articulate how they feel so they learn that emotions must be communicated in the right way. Do not allow the wrong behavior to set in and become natural or normal behavior to them because you are too tired to deal with it. Remember, it is a phase, once your children know that they will not get what they want by behaving badly, they will start to express themselves in a more positive way. It will get easier and easier until the right habits are formed and the bad ones are stamped out. I am sure you have heard of the terrible twos. Well, be assured that by being ruthless with our children's tantrums and habits, we did not have to put up with any such thing later, and neither will you.

6. Create Time to Unwind

Set times for your children to de-stress and unwind after school in accurate ways. Stress is a big part of children's lives today; they live in a different world to us. Try not to use words like *"when I was young..."* to discipline your child, but only to tell a story or something funny. When your child comes back from school, allow time for a favorite activity or something that allows the child to de-stress before the homework and chores come into play.

EXERCISE: Emotions and Money
Setting Right Emotions for Breakthrough

For Ages 5-8

Take your child to their favorite toy store. Tell your child that they can get a toy immediately. With this said, take them to a toy that you know is not their favorite, different and smaller. Next take them to their favorite section to a toy that you know that they like. Tell them that if they wait twelve weeks and work certain chores for those twelve weeks, you will get them this better toy, however, they may decide to get something smaller immediately if they choose not to wait.

You can repeat this exercise with the food that they like, a hobby they want to do, or anything else you choose. The rules are the same; if they wait and work for it, they get something better. This will build patience in them.

For All Ages

Plan some of your own exercises to build accurate emotional habits into your children.

Plan using these Questions as a guideline:

- What emotional habits do you need to build into your children?
  (Desired Outcome)

- How are you going to do this?
  (Method or Process)

- At what frequency (weekly/daily)?
  (Time Frame)

Use the chart on the following page to plan your exercises. Some sample exercises have been provided to get you started.

What emotional habits you need to build into your child?	How are you going to do this?	Frequency (Weekly Daily?)
Understanding that the world is all out to get them to spend. It is a game they can win if they don't give in.	Google 5 different advertisements with goods and services that are targeted to their age group. Explain to them how these organizations are subtly trying to get in their mind to get them to spend. Ask them how they are going to avoid being manipulated to spend by strangers. Work on setting a thinking pattern. These are the following thinking patterns you need to build in your child. 1. People always are in the game to get my money 2. Advertisements are not true and their trying to target and prey on young people like me and those who are emotionally week 3. I will respond only to purchase things after doing my research on benefits, comparisons with other products and price. 4. If I don't need it, I can keep money, invest it and become rich	1 advertisement per week.
The next time your child asks you for something that they want because their friends got the same thing. Get them to think whether they are making an informed decision for something they need or not.	Key questions to work on with your child: What are the other things they could get if they didn't buy this one thing? How much of their pocket money in percentage is going towards this product? What are they going to lose if they spend money like this every time they have an emotional impulse (give them real examples of celebrities, sportsmen and women who have gone broke because of a lack of money management)? Explain to them that they are playing a game and to win this game you have to be stronger than their emotional impulse. Once in a while, give them a smaller reward for not giving in (don't do this all the time as you will be feeding the emotional responses).	As often as your child asks for something due to comparing with what his friends have.

What emotional habits you need to build into your child?	How are you going to do this?	Frequency (Weekly Daily?)

Chapter 3

Wealth For a Cause

Giving Purpose and Meaning to Our Money

A cause is the scope of humanity or the world around you that you choose to improve by giving to it your time, your money and your energy. This is an area where change is needed and you are passionate about building and bringing that change.

Supporting a cause goes much more than just donating money. Donating money is the bare minimum and what we would consider the entry level.

Money as a Resource for Building a Cause

The principle of money for supporting or building a cause is one of the most important principles of Wealth and Finance. I am going to spend some time explaining this in detail.

Money is never for self. It is a resource. As with other resources, it is not an end unto itself, but a means to an end.

It must have a purpose. It must be able to take care of your needs and wants, but there must also be a purpose bigger than just yourself to which we can apply money. Many studies have shown that people who live a life that's bigger than themselves, thinking of those around them, their family, their community, and their nation, achieve greater impact that is lasting. Key business leaders today such as Bill Gates and Warren Buffet, two of the richest men in the world, have taken a pledge to give away huge portions of their wealth towards the betterment of society.

My question is, why do it only when you have reached the pinnacle of success? I am sure these business leaders would agree with me today, that it is always a great idea to start with the end in mind.

Imagine you are a young businessperson, just starting out in the business world and you are involved in a cause. You are using your time and experience, once a week, to teach children from disadvantaged communities to equip them with special skills, such as math or sports. Imagine that your business funds this cause.

Now imagine, that these children whom you coach or teach through the work you are doing with them have gained other values and skills which you impart such as drive, passion, a heart for others, your ability to organize, your ability to make the subject interesting and understandable for them. Imagine that all this results in four or five of these children becoming nation-changers, ministers in government, CEOs of corporations, etc. The possibilities of your own influence become limitless when it is poured out into others. Sometimes those from disadvantaged backgrounds just need a kick-start.

Let me give you another example. Our company, 'People Systems Consultancy' in Malaysia started taking up the cause of poverty eradication. We felt that everyone regardless of their background has the potential to provide for themselves. We didn't want to give loans to people and thereby have a hand in furthering their dependency on loans and debt. We also didn't believe education, or that the lack thereof, was an inhibitor for those people. So, we started training those with low education levels, even those who could not read and write.

We began to champion this cause by funding the initial projects ourselves; working with communities in need, training them, and monitoring their performance. Eventually other organizations such as the Government, Banks, and Corporations started to show an interest and began to ask if they could sponsor what we were doing because of the results we were getting.

At the time of writing this book, our company has trained 8, 000 people from low-income families. Many of them cannot read or write. The average income increase for those who undergo our program is between 100-400 percent per person. We have trained people from both rural and urban areas. We will be training another 10, 000 in the next three years' time.

Because of this cause our company has gained prominence. We have been asked to consult at government think-tank conferences. We also champion other causes such as financial literacy, which got us on prime time television and in major newspapers. Corporate training with a clear ROI to really bring change in companies is another cause of ours which got us into large corporations.

While the success and fame that came from championing this cause was not the reason we did it, it was a by-product of doing it. We really felt there was a need in our nation for someone to champion this cause, so we stood up even with limited resources and started small where we were. It has now become something that many organizations both big and small are partnering with us to accomplish.

In our company, we do stay true to our income generating activities such as corporate training and consultancy as this brings us revenue. We also use some of it to sponsor programs for those in need. However, the primary purpose of our business is for furthering the cause of transforming lives and communities and to be a contributor to nation building.

Now imagine what your child can become if he or she champions a cause with their finances, their business, their free time, or with the resources which they have.

Teach your children to live for a cause. My daughter, Mia, started her first business at the age of five and 50% of the money she earns goes towards the church building fund. She is as excited about her cause as she is about her business. She is now talking about giving a portion of her money, from her business, to an orphanage she visited recently.

I believe those who contribute their finances and their skills towards a cause are going to bring blessings upon their life, attract the best talent, create impact, and live meaningful lives.

Characteristics of a Cause

What is a cause? Here are a few distinctive characteristics that describe what a cause is:

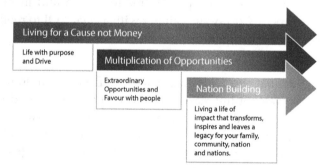

1. Centers Around Others Not You

A Cause is about others, not about you. This is something we must be clear about. You cannot claim that making yourself rich is a cause because as it is just about you. A cause is powerful for the reason that it is about others.

Some people may feel that their families could be a cause. While this is okay, it is not great. It is a very small world someone like that is living in. I believe a cause should be about society, our community, or our nation. National interest causes are great for us or our children to build into and champion. Technological improvement for humanity can be a cause. This could be what Alexander Graham Bell and Thomas Edison thought about when they invented what is making our lives more comfortable and easier today.

2. Centers Around Giving Not Getting

A Cause is not about what you can make out of it, it is about what you can give towards it. Never approach a cause by thinking about what you can get out of it. This will not get it moving or break any barriers.

Teach your children to be selfless and not selfish about their cause. Keep explaining that the cause will one day make a difference where they live. Point out situations that can change and sow the possibilities of exciting things that can happen. Children have active imaginations and if you stimulate it with the right inputs, there is no stopping how influential your child can become.

3. Requires a Contribution of Time

A Cause must be something you volunteer your time for, not something you do to get paid.

Be aware that rewards do come. Even volunteers gain rewards; they write a book, it becomes famous and they gain recognition from others. Rewards are fine, however, with a cause you must have the mindset of a volunteer. The rewards must be an added bonus, not the motivation you are doing the cause for. You must teach your child that if they do what is right in life they will attract rewards either in this life or the next. None of us live in a bubble. What each of us does touches others, so even if you do not believe there is an afterlife, teach your child to live in a way that creates impact. Make their life and yours count in the here and now. We have all heard about the "carbon footprint." I apply that thinking to something I like to call our "Impact Footprint". Did we really live a worthwhile life and leave a legacy behind that impacted our world and the people we share it with? Teach your child to live this way. When they live like this, they will inevitably leave a mark on their community and nation and become great (whether they receive recognition for what they are doing or not).

4. Engages One's Passion

A Cause is something you are able to be truly passionate about. We cannot take up a cause merely because we feel we can gain support for it. Neither can we take up a cause because others feel it is a good cause. We must be passionate about the cause we are applying ourselves to. Similarly, our children cannot take up a cause because we feel it is important. We can guide the decision but the decision must be theirs. It must be something they are passionate about. With younger children, this is sometimes difficult. We have to explain the cause, visually present it and excite them with the possibilities of the cause and what can happen. Also allow them to explore other causes if they change their mind. They will eventually pick something that is important to them.

They must carry a passion for the cause, because passion might be the only thing that sustains them in the future with the cause. They might have to fight difficulties, difficult people might attack them and attack the vision. There might be financial and other types of obstacles to overcome. It is the passion that will sustain them and break barriers to further the cause.

4. Willing to Pay the Price

A Cause is something you believe in enough to be willing to sacrifice for it. Our children must also learn that a cause is something for which they must be willing to sacrifice. They must be able to sacrifice time, give up things they like doing with their time to spend a bit of that time on the cause. They might have to give up money they could use to buy what they like, such as a toy or the latest technical device. No child is too young to make a sacrifice for what they believe in. The spirit of sacrificing for a cause will cause them to have drive that they can use in other important areas in their life such as, business, career, school, and many other situations or things in life where sacrifice is needed.

To get our children to understand the spirit of sacrifice we have to paint for them the picture of the rewards received by others who have sacrificed. More importantly we must be modeling this concept by living for a cause ourselves. Remember what I said earlier, we cannot preach what we do not practice.

5. Results in the Betterment of Humanity

A Cause is something that contributes towards the betterment of humanity and improves the lives of people. As I mentioned earlier, it does not only have to be about the poor or the needy, it can be about improving human lives through technological advancement.

My five year old daughter kept saying for a time that she wanted to invent a car that could fly so we could travel to destinations faster and with less traffic jams like we have in the city. I kept telling her it was a great idea, and started teaching her about science and technology. She lost interest after a while and now her cause is about raising money for our church building project. It's okay! Whatever your child wants to do, if it betters society in some way then let them do it and explore it.

If they want to create a shelter for dogs or animals and help improve living conditions for animals, that's fine too. Improving conditions for animals also brings betterment to humanity as we were put here on earth to steward the environment we cohabitate. It is our duty to improve conditions for animals and to improve conditions on our earth. Not to exploit animals and the earth. Taking up such a cause as the environment or animals will better humanity as we create a more sustainable planet

Let your children explore causes and change them when they are young. As they gain exposure, they will naturally settle on one that they can really build into. They can also do several things at one time, provided their priorities are agreed and settled upon. Their studies, moral and spiritual obligations must not be compromised.

Results of One's Involvement With a Cause

What will being involved in supporting a cause do for your children? What will it mean to them and develop in them? Here are some effects building a cause can have on an individual:

1. Engage the Law of the Universe

In life, what you give is what you get back. Many people do not realize that one of the foundations of financial management is growing our wealth by being generous to the right cause. Our wealth and that of the future of our children can come by hard work, discipline and many of the other principles in this book with which we can teach and prepare them, however, if they do not have a mindset of giving back to others, they will not attract wealth. The universe operates on the Law of Reciprocity.

We have all heard the phrases 'what goes around comes around,' 'you reap what you sow' or 'if you give, you get back' many times before. Can you think back in your life where you have seen this happen to you? I know I can. It is an important principle to teach to our children.

Let's take the rule further. When we give, we get back and

sometimes (and most often) not necessarily from the same source we gave it to. Our reward can come from anywhere and anyone.

This is one of my firm beliefs in life. My goal is to give, my best, my money, and my time to those who need it without worrying about what I get back in return. Of course I pursue my work for my work is a cause. Educating those who are in poverty and helping them come out of it by financially educating adults, youth and children so that they can live free is my cause. Wealth is a by-product of our cause.

2. Presents a Platform for Achieving Success

Being involved with a cause gives an opportunity for a child to achieve success, and success is contagious. It can transfer to other areas.

Most of life's success revolves around something that people are passionate about. Teaching our children how to drive the right passions and to succeed in them is something that having and working for a cause will automatically do for our children.

When they work for a cause, our children have to stretch themselves, they have to go beyond their comfort zones, overcome obstacles, and drive through countless situations where their limits of motivation will be stretched. A cause is one of the best educators of success because we have to drive it, and we have to influence others which is important. There are no shortcuts. We have to build it with all the energy we have.

Our children will be able to discover the potential they have within themselves; confidence will build, and so will drive. What actually is forming is character and the ability to bring these new found characteristics such as drive, confidence, the ability to overcome obstacles, and the ability to convince people into everything they work on.

It will become automatic. Our character traits don't live in isolation. They are part of us, they are the real us and translate into everything we do. The same thing will happen for the success traits that we build in our children by using the cause as a vehicle to do it.

3. Creates a Sense of Self-Worth

Being part of a cause creates a strong sense of self-worth through a meaningful life that contributes to society. Many people I grew up with whom I admired and thought had the greatest potential in life are now working mundane 9-5 type jobs and are unhappy with their lives. When your life makes a difference to others you will be a happy person. A cause can be a legacy we leave behind for humanity. It doesn't have to be larger than life. We don't need publicity for what we are doing. Those things are low measures of impact. The true standard is what we have done with our own life and what we have built into our children so that they achieve with their lives a measure that far exceeds the expectations of their potential, and that they have impacted others while doing so. We may not be a Martin Luther King who impacts millions, but it's okay, because we can still impact 2, 000 people through a cause we believe in, are passionate about, and work with. We have left a legacy behind, and contributed to humanity.

Robert Kyosaki once said that as a C grade student he was doing better in life and achieving more than those who were academically different. Our society has evolved so much from meaningful standards, and our children are being told that their measure of success is not what they do for others but their grades in school and in university. Don't get me wrong, it is still important to get good grades, stay in school and achieve results. It helps you in numerous ways. However, think of the cause you are building in your child as an extra-curricular activity that builds self-worth, confidence, and the ability to impact others. It makes them live a worthwhile and fulfilling life.

Our children's self-worth must be more than just academic

results and money. These things are important by-products of life, but their self-worth must come from who they are and how they have served the human race.

4. Cultivates a Missionary Mentality of Contentment

When our children have a well-informed worldview and are living to support a cause, they will be living for more than just their own needs. The missionary mentality learned by serving a cause, allows your child to be flexible and to live within his means and overcome difficult times easily. People who live for a cause become like missionaries, they live in a frugal way that is contented with what are the necessities of their life, but they don't pay much attention to status objects that others just "have to buy" or strive for to feel a sense of worth. They already have their fulfillment, self-worth and reason for living coming from the cause they support. They don't need to be like the rest of society who strive for status and objects to compensate for their lack of self-worth.

If you can afford something and have access to it, there is nothing wrong with enjoying a bit of luxury. So I am not talking about giving all your money away and living like a monk. Some things are necessary when we move up in society and do business in certain circles - for example - we can't take clients to street vendors for a lunch meeting, but need a good restaurant where we can talk.

The problem with luxury goods, like we dealt with in chapter two is that most people who cannot afford it, strive to get it by using money they don't have, to have a lifestyle they cannot afford, to impress people they don't know. The emotional trigger to compulsively buy higher than your means is an emotional lack that children who have been trained to support a cause from a young age will not be affected by. Their sense of self-worth already comes from what they are championing and how they are supporting and contributing value to it. They do not need to impress anybody. They are living for something bigger than just themselves.

5. Adds Greater Meaning to Life

A life well lived is a life that has contributed to humanity and improved the lives of others. Whatever our cause may be; whether it is technology, a social cause, community improvement projects or the environment, the cause will be something that our children can look back on and be proud of because of their 'Impact Footprint' here on earth.

Many people look back on their life with regret, they start thinking about contributing to others too late. Our children can and will have a head start in leaving their mark.

How does this have a bearing on financial education you ask? Financial intelligence is not a stand-alone thing. True financial intelligence does not only take into account our own financial standing, but also that of those around us who are in need. Values associated with financial intelligence play a big part in how we use our money, how we earn it, and what we do with our harvest or millions when we practice these principals diligently.

Don't let your child be like those who start thinking about others too late. Set them on the right path from day one. Also teach them balance. They must not be religious in their giving; meaning that they give away everything religiously yet have their families live in lack.

A cause is something both a husband and wife share and discuss together and plan towards. How much of your resources or your pay check supports the cause? How much time do you want to spend on it? How do you educate your children with it? Come to an agreement and then begin to implement what you have planned. Give your child a life of no regrets by starting them early on the right path.

It would be time well-spent putting some thought into what our children can support as a cause.

EXERCISE: Wealth for a Cause
Giving Purpose and Meaning to Our Money

For All Ages

Answer these questions to help your child define their cause:

1. What is the cause that your child can champion?

   (For children aged 5-7 explain a cause as helping others or those around them.)

2. Who is it benefiting from it? (individuals, groups, communities, charities, nation)

3. How is it benefiting them?

4. What is your child's passion?

5. Can your child's passion be used as a cause?

6. What should your child sacrifice for the cause?

7. What % of the child's income (allowance, gift money, pocket money, or other income) is your child going to use to support the cause?

8. Can your child raise money for the cause? What can he or she do?

Use the table on the next page to track how well your child is working with the cause.

Actions	Frequency	Successes achieved

Chapter 4

Wealth Acquisition Principles

Essential Foundations for a Lifetime of Wealth

Principles of Wealth

There are two kinds of principles of wealth, Wealth Acquisition Principles and Wealth Management Principles.

Wealth Acquisition Principles

These are the principles of wealth that help you to acquire wealth.

- Principle of Tithing
- Principle of Accountability and Oversight
- Principle of Honoring Your Parents
- Principle of Wealth for a Purpose

Wealth Management Principles

These are the principles of wealth that help you to manage and retain the wealth that you acquire.

- Principle of Budgeting
- Principle of Expense Tracking
- Principle of Investment
- Principle of Debt Management

We will cover the Wealth Management Principles that help you and your child to manage and retain your wealth in later chapters in this book. However, in this chapter we are going to deal with the first group of wealth principles.

This first group of wealth principles is key because it will set you up with a proper foundation for a lifetime of wealth acquisition. You may have all the knowledge and behavior of the second group of principles, but if you are not pulling in the money, both you and your children will have your wealth building goals stifled.

Process Flow Activated by Wealth Acquisition Principles

This is the process flow for us to open the gates of wealth in our children and in our own lives.

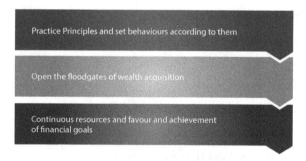

Practice Principles and set behaviours according to them

Open the floodgates of wealth acquisition

Continuous resources and favour and achievement of financial goals

Wealth Acquisition Principles

True wealth is a result of accurate behavior and an accurate life. In becoming wealthy and achieving success, it is not the results that matter as much as it is how we got there and how we achieved it. Our testimony of this process is paramount. We need to set behavioral principles in our lives that help us acquire wealth.

There are many rich people who practice the right principles and who are examples of virtue in their community. They became rich by doing right and living right. The last thing we want is for our children to become wealthy yet live by wrong principles and have a bad testimony. It is imperative that our children understand important principles of wealth acquisition so that they have these inbuilt into their lives.

The following are key universal operational principles that can bring a person into wealth and success. These principles are critical and must be built into our children to form part of their ethos and character.

I believe all success in life is built upon principles. We cannot become wealthy from a poor state of finances without hard work. It is a principle. Neither can we live long without proper exercise and diet. While some may say, "*Then, all common sense are principles and we don't really need to learn specific principles. We can just follow common sense, right?*"

Well, you couldn't be more wrong. Many people to whom I have taught financial intelligence have somehow or other forgotten these principles, or did not know and understand the importance thereof and therefore did not practice them. Others did not prioritize them and so lapsed in their initial practice of them.

The key about these principles is that they must be built into our children until they have become a set of values and habits they live by. This will ensure that our children practice them and stay out of trouble.

THE PRINCIPLE OF TITHING

Tithing is a powerful way of keeping the proverbial 'windows of heaven' open over our lives.

It deals, again, in the universal principle or law of reciprocity, whereby before you are able to receive, you are first to give.

If you continually want to remain and live on the receiving end, it is only reasonable that you put in place in your life a working principle, or system, that allows you to be giving on a consistent and continual basis. What I refer to as "Tithing" is such a system.

The traditions of many of the major people-groups and religious groups of the world advocate the principle of gifting a tithe. For example; the Hebrew concepts of *Terumah* and *Ma'aser*, the Islamic concepts of *Zakat* and *Usher*, the Christian concepts of *Tithes* and *Offerings*, The Sikh concept of *Daswandh*, the historical Middle-Eastern *Masretu* all relate to giving (often a tenth) in recognition of a 'Higher Power.' Even the world famous financial guru, Robert Kiyosaki, talks about tithing of your income to charity in his best-selling book *"Rich Dad Poor Dad"* as an important principle that releases wealth.

What is important is that we recognize the universality of the principle and activate its operation in our lives.

For me the rule is to give away 10% of our income. By doing this I have seen major blessings released in my life and that of my family.

What is Tithing?

Tithing is an act of showing honor for a spiritual source through the giving of 10% of our income in recognition of that source. It can be done by giving the tithe to a spiritual leader or those that represents your spiritual source, who is like a resource or storehouse to you, or alternatively just giving it to charity.

If we are not tithing in honor of our spiritual source, there is a big chance we are missing the opportunity to sow into something that can reap us a harvest.

Benefit of Tithing

I am often asked, "What is the benefit of tithing?" I cannot speak for others, but I am going to show you the blessings that happened to me when I started tithing to the right source (tithing, but not to the right person or the right source might not do anything much for you). The right source is important as it is like a storehouse, a continuous resource for your life.

Through practicing the accurate principles and teachings that you received from this 'storehouse' you have grown mentally, emotionally, spiritually and financially, (if your storehouse or religious organization has the capacity to do this for you).

My storehouse is my church and I tithe 10% of my income to it. I also give offerings above and beyond my tithes to the Ministries of Dr Jonathan David, whose teachings are a major resource for me.

We must recognize that tithing is a principle practiced and taught in every major religion across the world. Those with spiritual awareness will know that God does not need our money, but we honor God by giving of our time to serve and our money to do good for others.

If you do not subscribe to an established norm of tithing, you can tithe to a charity or a cause that you support and that resonates with you. It does not have to be a religious body. It is, however, important to tithe to your storehouse from where you draw resources for your life.

It is good for both you and your children to have a storehouse that you contribute towards, but as I said, if you do not have one, find a charity or a cause that speaks to you and tithe there.

The principle of tithing is a fundamental universal principle that must be taught to every child, as practicing it can bring them into supernatural blessings. Let me share with you some of the blessings that happened in my own life (I don't have space for all of them, and I want to contextualize it to finance) so that you can decide for yourself whether you want your children and yourself to access such blessings.

As mentioned before, it is not about our preferred system of belief or religion, it is recognizing a universal financial principle, that when practiced, brings a financial harvest.

Blessings on My Family Due to Tithing

Here are some of the blessings that my family and I have received as a result of putting the Principle of Tithing to practice:

1. An Assurance of Divine Favor

I have peace and joy in what I do and my family is one that is blessed with peace as well. It is not that we don't have struggles. I am running a multinational company with over 30 highly capable employees. This takes time and energy to drive things and work things out. Sometimes there are delays, problems with people and all the other situations that business people have to face.

One of my key employees once asked, *"I can see God blessing you and you don't carry a lot of stress, what is your secret?"*

Yes, I face many of the same things many other business owners face, but I have an edge that they do not have. I believe I have the blessings of God. These are blessings that come with no stress and no other lack.

2. Supernatural Connections for Business

We have somehow always met the right people at the right time. It has not just happened once or twice, but consistently.

Even my staff has remarked when I've asked them to call a client to speak to them about a particular program we have, *"How did you know they needed exactly that?"*

It is not just a sixth sense. I believe it is a blessing that comes from tithing my income to my storehouse. One of my biggest clients over the last five years came from a supernatural connection when I was put on stage with him to be a conference speaker at a women's economic empowerment conference. We are still working together five years on and the relationship has resulted in large contracts for us time and time again. Of course we have been diligent to deliver results as well, but the connection itself started at that conference.

You may think it is one time, but I can go on and on sharing and can fill up a chapter on the supernatural connections we have had. Right time and Right place seems to happen to us all the time. Do you think it's normal or we are just lucky? I don't believe in luck but supernatural connections.

Imagine what the principle of tithing can do for your children?

3. Accelerated Growth in Business Revenue

Our company 'People Systems,' experienced 300% growth in revenue in our first three years. It was unbelievable. Many people, including our accountant at the time, commented that this was not growth that any others in our industry experienced.

One accountant said. *"Tell me the truth Raymond, you guys are not just doing training right? You must be doing other types of businesses. I audit training companies, they do not achieve these types of revenue."*

Our revenue has continued to accelerate. We have years where we don't achieve our targets, but revenues even at those times are high and we always seem to bounce back. We have never lacked (also because we keep our lifestyle low). Again, this is an important principle that when practiced, your child will also begin to reap the rewards of.

They will grow faster and be more stable financially than their peers.

4. Extraordinary Protection in Business and Life

The one thing that most people would dream of is always having the right advice come to you at the right time, or the right feeling to do something. This type of protection from dangerous situations and counsel in situations with the potential to gain from, in both our business and in life, is what we have come to experience. I believe it is as a result of tithing to our storehouse.

I recently felt I should buy Apple shares. My broker felt that it was not a good share to buy; it wasn't exciting enough. I insisted. The inner voice that was guiding me was strong and confident. So he bought it and a few weeks later, apple announced they were going for a share split. The share went up and I made a good profit.

I don't have any inside information, I am in Malaysia and I do not know anyone in apple. There is an inner voice that guides me that tells me what to do and most of the time, (almost always) it has been right.

I am blessed with relationships that have come to me and given me great advice at just the right time when I needed it; To sell my first business and move into what I am doing now, to buy my house before the prices went up, and many other things that have resulted in financial blessings.

I have also had advice that protected me. The advice to stay away from someone came just at the right time when I was about to go into partnership with that person.

I am enjoying a wonderful marriage. I was guided to my

wife and I am enjoying blessing in my relationship and I see other people don't in their marriage.

These are results that most parents want for their children. That they would be protected and taken care of and have the right counsel, even when parents are not around. Tithing can bring your child that, either through an inner voice that will guide them or friends and people around them who will tell them what they need to hear, guide them and protect them.

5. No Financial Lack

My wife and I have reached that place of being down and out before we had become financially blessed and have no fear of lack of money. At that time we were not as financially free as we are now, but we just knew in our hearts and minds that as we began to honor God with our tithe, we would have no lack. Sure enough through all these years whenever we had a need, we had enough money to meet it, not just for ourselves but for others as well.

Tithing can bring your child into a place that they will have no lack. This happens in two areas. Firstly, there is peace in their heart and a knowing that they will have no lack, and secondly, they will physically have no lack when it comes to money. Every need of theirs will be met (notice I say need not want, as we sometimes desire ridiculous things that can derail us). Whatever they need for life, things like a decent car for work, a house to live in, enough healthy food to eat, everything like that will be in the hands of the child and adult who tithes.

6. Children with Intelligence and Spiritual Awareness

I believe that the gift of children who are blessed with extraordinary intelligence and spiritual awareness, and who live according to good moral values are also released into our lives as a result of tithing.

My daughter tithes her income, allowance, and savings

to the church and my pastor still keeps her first envelop of her tithe that she gave when she was three. My daughter is blessed with extraordinary intelligence and while I believe my wife and I are good parents, and have taken a keen interest in and have actively worked on her development, she is showing ability beyond her years.

She recently went for a written assessment test for a private school. She was in pre-school at the time and was supposed to be assessed for level one. Even though she was mistakenly assessed for level two in Math and English, she still scored 82 and 84 out of one hundred respectively. When I talk to her and explain things, she is blessed with an extraordinarily quick mind and intellect that enables her to move fast and understand things faster than many others.

In addition to her development plan that my wife and I have thought through and implemented, I believe that her own tithing has also brought blessings into her life. She is well liked by teachers and students alike, and does well in whatever she is asked to do.

In Summary

I know what I just shared above might sound unbelievable, but I ask, what's the point of writing a book to share secrets on how to raise your children to be millionaires or financially free if I keep the best secret to myself? Try the principle, and see what happens to you when you practice it. As said before, this is not a matter of religion. Regardless of your spiritual beliefs, blessings will come into your life if you practice accurate principles. Find a charity, a cause or a storehouse that you want to contribute to and support and give 10% of your income there.

I believe that this is my secret to success, and to the blessings in my life → Tithing.

Calculating Your Tithe

- The principle is for you to give 10% of your **income**, taken off the top. For example if you are earning $10, 000 your tithe will be $1, 000

- If you have a business and your turnover is USD $100, 000, your profit might be $40, 000 to you personally. Your tithe is then $4, 000.

====================== PRINCIPLE TWO ======================
THE PRINCIPLE OF ACCOUNT- ABILITY AND OVERSIGHT

The principle of accountability and oversight can be practiced for big purchase decisions with a spouse, if you are married, or a leader or mentor that you trust in the area of finance.

Most of us will have problem areas where we like to spend money. Mine are what I call 'guy things,' which are basically, watches, pens, and leather goods. Yet one of the things that I have learned to do in order to deal with them is to have oversight; my wife.

I don't buy things to reward myself unless one of my sources of multiplication of income generates enough for me to reinvest more and also has a small portion I can use for rewarding myself. However, irrespective of whether this condition is met, my money boss, (my wife) has the final say. This sense of accountability is a principle we need to teach our children, but more importantly they need to see us model this behavior first.

Who is your money boss? Or do you make every purchase decision unilaterally by yourself? Our children need to understand that we are careful and check our decisions with others before we purchase things.

There are a few ways you can be accountable with money:

Get a Money Boss

I have already explained this concept earlier with how I check with my wife before I reward myself. If she says no, then I abide by that. My children begin to see a model of accountability that they can practice as well. When I explain the concept of a money boss they will already understand it better because they have seen it in action.

A money boss is someone you trust with whom you discuss unneeded purchases, purchases that could be considered as rewards. If you are not sure if it is a reward check with your money boss! We also need to be clear that the money boss provides some accountability and oversight, they do not exercise control over your finance. Your money boss does not have to hold your money, you hold it, but their OPINION is what matters. It is good if it is someone you respect and whose opinion matters to you.

It is important to teach what makes a good money boss to your children so that they can pick the right type of person for their own money boss.

The criteria for a money boss is as follows:

1. Good with Personal Financial Management

A money boss is someone who is good at personal financial management and may or may not be related to you.

A money boss does not have to be a spouse or family member, especially if the background where relatives come from has underlying bad money habits, as this is only going to compound your problems. It must be someone who is already practicing the right habits with their own money. They do not have to be a genius with money, just someone who is established in good habits with money.

2. Trustworthy and Comfortable

A money boss is someone whom you trust and are comfortable with. You will be talking with your money boss on topics that are very important to you. It might be that you will need to reveal sensitive personal details relevant to your financial habits to your money boss. Therefore you need to choose someone who will not betray your trust or take advantage of you. This needs to be thoroughly explained to your child. Most children, especially teenagers, have a mindset that if they like someone, that person must be good and therefore can be trusted. This cannot be further from the truth. They need someone with some backbone and character and who has been seen to practice good financial habits, but also someone they can be comfortable sharing with who will not take advantage of them.

3. Sound and Honest Opinions

Your money boss must not be afraid of saying what needs to be said. If your money boss is heavily influenced by you and follows everything you want, then that's a money friend, not a money boss. A money boss needs to be able to be firm with you and give you their honest opinion in a clear and direct way. They cannot be afraid of telling you the truth.

Reward Reaching Financial Targets

You should structure rewards to be had only once a financial target is reached. This is the second thing you can teach your child about being accountable with money. They should not reward themselves all the time but only on special occasions and certain times. More importantly these times should only be when they achieve a financial target.

For example, with a child you can say, "*If you save up to this amount, we as your parents will top up some money and allow you to get this small reward.*" (Do not encourage them to splurge everything they save. A large portion must be kept aside to continue saving.)

If they understand the psychology that they will be rewarded if they save, then they will also understand that they will be rewarded in life if they save.

This is one of the things that I practice. I normally set targets for my investments. For example, if I buy a share there should be a targeted entry and exit price. When the share exceeds that, then I have a surplus. If, let's say, there is a period where all my investments exceed my expectations, then I know I can take out a small portion from the excess (not from the initial capital) let's say 2 % and I can then give myself or my family a small reward.

If you use this concept in the training of your child, you will give them saving goals, lifestyle goals, and business goals (you are never too young to start a business), and then you can reward your child with a small portion of the returns (not the capital) when it comes.

The idea is to structure rewards. In fact, in most cases where people have problems it is because they do not reward themselves in a structured way, and then they splurge because they are frustrated.

As mentioned in chapters One and Two, you must also teach your child to enjoy rewards that do not entail shopping, buying goods, or spending money.

Earn Your Rewards

Another good mindset to teach your child in terms of accountability with money is to get them to earn rewards for the completion of major productive and purposeful tasks. Not just give it to themselves whenever they feel like it.

When I write and finish a book, which I have to do in between running a couple of businesses, I then give myself a good reward with a local holiday or a dinner at a restaurant I enjoy.

This ensures that I am productive and also enjoying the fruits of my labor, not fruits of desire. This is a very important distinction to make.

To build accountability with your children they must appreciate that rewards are special, but they can earn them by hard work and labor and reward themselves for completion of their goals.

=============== PRINCIPLE THREE ===============
THE PRINCIPLE OF HONORING YOUR PARENTS

One of the most difficult things I have to continuously do in training some audiences is to convince them that honoring their parents is an important principle for wealth building.

Previous generations seems to have been more willing to accept the responsibility to take care of their parents and saw it as being honorable to do so. In this generation more and more people have been adopting the mindset that parents should take care of themselves or move into a nursing home.

There are exceptions to every situation of course, and I am not saying all nursing homes are bad, or that putting your parents there is the wrong thing to do, it may be the right thing. However, honoring our parents by taking care of them or giving to them from your income is based on universal principles.

For example, if a son or daughter of an elderly parent has a situation where both the child and their spouse work, and the elderly person is impaired and cannot walk without assistance, then it may be dangerous to leave such a person alone at home as there might be a risk of serious injury to the elderly parent. In such a case a professional home that takes care of the elderly in a proper and honorable way is very important and necessary. There are other medical situations where this is needful and there could also be situations whereby some mental health issues dictate that having your parents stay with you becomes untenable.

We are not just talking about the issue of nursing homes, but about using our money to honor our parents and to take care of them in their old age.

We need to model taking care of our parents and teach this to our children, regardless of our own relationship situation with our parents.

This Can be Thought of in the Following Manner; Just Do It!

1. Regardless of Agreement in Relationship

It does not matter if you don't see eye to eye or agree with your parents, just do it anyway.

Some people argue that they have never seen eye to eye with their parents, therefore they feel they do not need to take care of them and provide for them financially. They argue that this would mean that their parents win. It is viewed that because they are giving the parents money when not agreeing on major issues they are losing this battle and the parents are winning.

If they are using the money you are giving them for harmful or silly and extreme purposes such as supporting some terrorist group that's blowing people up mindlessly, then you should create a trust account for them and not give them the money directly. This trust account should provide them with comfort and a reasonable lifestyle and be governed according to your predetermined conditions. It should pay for medical expenses or needs that they have, such as a new car or proper living quarters. Basically, it provides everything they NEED and gives them some comfort from their wants as well.

2. Regardless of Past Bad Parenting

It does not matter if you consider them to have been lousy parents, just do it anyway.

Regardless if they were lousy parents to you, or if they were not around when you needed them, or cheated on their spouse, you need to honor them because it is a principle.

When we look at our parents, there are so many things that they have done wrong and in hindsight they could have done better or maybe even learnt more. You may have the education and the insight they did not have. All this does not matter; don't live from your hurt, but live from accurate convictions and principles and teach your children to do this as well.

Most people feel that if their parents made bad mistakes, they do not have to talk to them or work with them. They carry this unforgiveness and eventually pass these bad habits on to their children.

This unforgiveness begins to eat them up and allows other negative influences and thoughts to come in. Keep your mind free of negative emotions, thoughts and feelings. You will have better health, a better mind, and attract wealth. Negative emotions attract other negative emotions, thoughts and actions. My mentor always says when speaking about this context, *"Don't steal from the mafia!"*

Let's teach this to our children as well. Most people live

with emotional wounds and scars from their past caused by their parents. These are what I call *'wealth inhibitors'* and *'life inhibitors'*. The full life that we and also our children could have enjoyed would be cut short because of negativity, fear and resentment that have built up over many years.

The key is to free ourselves of this and then teach our children how to free themselves as well.

You can free yourself from the wealth and life inhibitors by doing this:

- Learn to forgive and let go.

- Learn to visualize good things (positives) and not bad things (negatives) that your parents did for you.

- Learn to move in circles and have friends that are positive towards negative situations. Birds of a feather flock together. This, I'm sure, you have heard, so don't be a negative bird.

- Learn how to handle the negativity of others by preparing earlier. By this I mean to be prepared for them acting in a negative way and resolve not to give in to their negativity by matching their negative responses. Walk away or think of something positive.

3. Regardless of Past Lack of Provision

It does not matter that they didn't give you everything (financially) you think you deserved, just do it anyway. Maybe you have resentment towards your parents because they squandered money and did not give you the education or opportunities you feel you deserved. Maybe they didn't get you that toy you wanted. Guess what? We are going to disappoint our children with their wants as well. We will not be able to get them everything they want because sometimes what they want is not good for them.

Maybe you even felt that some of your friends in the same income category were getting things that you were not. It does not matter!

4. Regardless of Current Spending

It does not matter what they do with the money you are giv-ing them. Except if they are mentally unstable, put the money in a trust account for them, and make the trust responsible for taking care of them. Otherwise, just do it anyway.

Why Financially Honoring Your Parents is Important for Wealth Building?

1. What Goes Around, Comes Around

If we are carrying unforgiveness towards our parents and treat-ing them badly, our children are picking this up as a value. When they disagree with us, and they will, they will treat us in the same way as they have learned from watching how we treat our parents.

Children observe adult behavior and take them as normal behavior. Studies have shown that children, who grow up in violent abusive households where spouses treat each other that way, even if they are not abusive towards their children, later feel that being abusive is the way they should treat their own spouse.

Not honoring your parents, as I have mentioned, is a wealth inhibitor. If we can teach and model for our children practices and habits that are wealth accumulators rather than inhibitors in their lives, this becomes something that empow-ers them to attract wealth throughout their entire life.

This is also true when it comes to our children picking up key points and practices to model for their own children. These habits must go to our posterity (the next and ensuing generations), so that all who come after us will be blessed.

2. To Model Using Wealth for What is Honorable

It is vitally important for our children to see us using our wealth for honorable purposes. They must see us using money for honorable purposes and such charitable causes as, supporting the poor, taking care of family members in need and others. In this context most important that money should not ONLY be used just to make more money, but it should also be used to further a cause and help those in need.

If our children see their parent being one who uses money for honorable purposes, this becomes a value in them and they begin to use their own money in the same way.

My daughter asked me recently whether she could contribute to an orphanage she visited the year before when she was four years old, from the proceeds of her business. She is not only thinking of doing business for herself, and her own needs, but using money for honorable purposes. These are practices and principles that attract wealth just like honoring our parents with our money is a principle that will help our children attract wealth.

Although it could be an uncomfortable principle to teach your child, it is an important one. You are not serving your own needs when you do this, think accurately, you are giving your children the principles to attract wealth to themselves.

3. To Model a Good Testimony

When your wealth is also used to take care of your parents you become a model citizen with a good testimony. Many people become rich, but do not have a good testimony. We must never lose our testimony when we become wealthy. One of the fastest ways for us, or our children, to lose it is to treat those close to us, our family, our parents, and our children, with dishonor when it comes to money.

How many times have we read in the papers where members of prominent families, children or parents, take each other to court fighting over money, or are not using their wealth to take care of their own parents and children, thereby having news coverage of a bad testimony?

If parents and children (and also other family members) know how to honor we can keep our testimony clean. Ultimately our testimony is what keeps people interested in working with us and joining with us for business and life, and more importantly, it keeps wealth flowing into our lives.

4. To Honor Your Parents

We also honor our parents with our money simply for the sake of honoring our parents for being our parents. There is so much that we need to teach our children, and remembering that we must practice it first, how do we do this?

Decide and take action to give your parents 10% of your income. If you really can't because you are in a bad financial situation, then work out a budget allocating what you can afford to give them. Be consistent with that portion.

You also have to work towards taking care of the following of your parents' needs:

- Medical Expenses

  Buy insurance coverage for them if they do not have enough or use a portion of your cash

- Housing

- Proper Nutrition and Diet

  Especially if they need to be on a prescribed diet for health reasons

- Proper Care

  Get the appropriate care such as, nurses or maids, if they need it

- Entertainment Activities and Holidays for their Recreation

- Quality of Life

  Any other basic ingredient in their lifestyle, or for a better lifestyle, that you can afford to give them

When I achieved my wealth, I helped my parents with the renovation for their home, medical expenses, down-payments for their car, household expenses, emergency funds, appliances for their home to upgrade their lifestyle, and many other things so that their needs could be met. This is in addition to taking care of them financially and given them money every month.

THE PRINCIPLE OF WEALTH FOR A PURPOSE

Wealth must have a purpose, not be the purpose in and of itself. There is a fine line between living and managing wealth to grow a cause and to live life to the fullest, and living just to make more money for yourself and your own needs.

Money must be for a purpose bigger than ourselves, and the purpose of life cannot just be for ourselves and for our own needs. What then should be the purpose for our wealth?

Here are some ingredients that the right type of purpose will have and do:

1. Excite You

Our purpose for wealth should be something that excites us and drives us to work harder, live a moderate lifestyle and become a better person. Our purpose should not be just about ourselves and our own goals and needs. It must be something that causes us to work harder, drives us with excitement and creates momentum for us or our children to practice the right financial habits.

Getting our purpose right can evolve over time. For example, a five year old child might have a very different purpose for wealth than an adolescent.

Our child's purpose or even our own purpose can evolve with the growth and progress of our self-awareness, our personal and spiritual development.

There might be new important fields, areas or goals in our lives at different stages and it is okay to evolve with them. Our purpose is different from a cause, which can also change over time, in that our purpose can change more frequently to suit our age, and stature at different points in our lives. Purpose is normally a subset to a cause in life. Meaning, there can be a few purposes that help articulate your cause in different areas.

2. Require Engaged Energy and Thought

Our purpose is something that we have to give energy and thought to consistently. Because it is a purpose we cannot be supporting it or working it in the background or when we have time. It has to be at the forefront of our life, our time, and what we use our money for.

When it comes to our purpose, both we and our children have to reflect, from time to time, whether we are achieving this and living it. We also have to gauge at different stages whether our purpose is still relevant to the stage of life we are in.

We must also help our children to do this. For example, at age five your child might be deeply moved by an orphanage she visited, as my daughter was, and wants one of the purposes for the money she earns to be contributing towards this orphanage.

There could also be other purposes later on. She might want to support a learning development center or a shelter for battered women. Her cause remains the same, which is to use money to improve the lives of humanity and transform communities, but she has different purposes under the cause umbrella that she works or grows into.

3. Help Others

Our purpose is something that is always about helping others and empowering them, not just donating to a charity, if it is possible. Many people need to understand it is not just donating money to others or charities that gives us a fulfilling life. It is empowering people. Our children need to understand this. There are plenty of rich people who donate tons of money and still live an unfulfilled life. Money must be a means to an end, not the end in itself. If it is the end in itself, we are in the rat race. I believe neither we, nor our children, are RATS! or hamsters on a wheel. When I say purpose and driving it, this sometimes involves not just the giving of money, but more importantly the giving of oneself in time and energy.

If your purpose or that of your child is to empower children in orphanages for example, it is insufficient for your child to just give a portion of their own money to the cause. They must also volunteer their time and energy. They need to go there to help, to serve, to teach or to clean up the place.

There are two important things everyone has in life that they will be held accountable for; Time and Money. I believe we are to teach our children to handle both well and to be accountable for it, to make it count, is what I want to say (which means that both are used to make a difference in the lives of others).

4. Support a Cause

The purpose of money should be to support the cause of the purpose you are building. Money itself should not be your reason for living.

Many Parents especially in the Asian families, tell their children *"Go to school, study hard, don't have too much fun, go to university, study law, medicine or engineering, come out, work hard and earn lots of money and repeat the cycle with your own children."*

A lot of children from Asian families have been through this with their parents and are fed up. They are looking for meaning; life is more than just money. Basically, Asian cultures in the past have lived in conditions where survival was something to be fought for every day. As conditions improved and these families began to acquire moderate lifestyles and some wealth, they were not fighting anymore and so a life with meaning, not just a life with wealth, came to be more important.

It is imperative for all parents, Asian or not, to teach their children, not just to strive for gaining wealth, but to also live their lives with purpose and meaning by living for others (by living a life bigger than themselves).

Some Examples of Purposes for Money

Impacting disadvantaged children in orphanages through education	Championing sports and character for children to learn	Working with animals to provide shelter and homes
Saving the environment by recycling and promoting alternative lifestyles	Having a spirit of improving human lives through systems, processes	Creating avenues for disadvantaged youth to gain scholarships
Using science to better peoples lives	Community service to the underprivileged and homeless in your community	Bringing out artistic talent through dance, music with underprivileged youth

Your child can have more than one purpose and can try different things, but remember, they can also change it if they want to move on to something else.

I used examples of youth and children so that you could work with your own children to find out what could be purposes that suit them.

NOTE: if your children are involved, the purpose must be safe for them and you. Be careful with the areas and situations you get involved in. I used to volunteer to rehabilitate drug addicts off the street, to bring them to hospitals, rehab centres and spend time counseling them. As time went by I built up trust with them. They lived in alleyways, drainage areas and many other places in the city they could find shelter. However, these are not areas I would rush to take my children to at ages 3-5. I might when they are older, and more aware and capable of understanding that some of these areas can be dangerous, but you have to gauge what safety measures are in the best interest of your own family.

EXERCISE: Wealth Acquisition Principles
Essential Foundations for a Lifetime of Wealth

For All Ages

Plan how you are going to teach and model these Principles of Wealth to your children using the template on the next page.

As your children grow older, you will have to delve deeper into these concepts and teach them more extensively.

Principle	How you are going to communicate it?	How you are going to model it for them to see it?	How you are going to teach it to them?
The Principle of Tithing			
The Principle of Accountability and Oversight			
The Principle of Honouring Your Parents			
The Principle of Wealth for a Purpose			
Other Important Principles You Hold			

Chapter 5

Setting a Budget
Planning and Living for Wealth Acquisition

Accurate Budgeting for Differentiated Savings

Never put all your eggs in one basket. This is so true and the same can be said for not putting all your savings in one account. Many parents have told their children, *"you need to save,"* and *"savings are important."* So why is it then that we never saved enough? Or why is it that people live lifestyles that are not commensurate with their incomes? The reason behind this is that the concept of wealth multiplication and wealth generation is not taught as an important concept to children. We need a fresh and accurate approach to budgeting and savings. This chapter will show the importance of setting up your budget with different savings baskets.

To truly become wealthy, children must live a wealth multiplier lifestyle. Savings are a by-product of that lifestyle. Savings are not the end in itself. With all the messages bombarding our children telling them to spend their money, they need compelling reasons to save. Multiplying wealth to achieve goals and living for a cause are such reasons.

We have to educate our children that the reasons for budgeting and saving are to achieve their financial goals and to support their cause. They need to see the link between these or else they won't have the conviction to do it.

Build a compelling case first, before you give them the tools in this chapter then teach them about budgeting and tracking.

One important note here is that they must feel they are able to achieve wealth. We have to believe in them and believe in ourselves when we are modeling it.

Most people do not want to live for a better future because they don't see that there is one possible. Build hope into your children, give them a life that is impactful through instilling the lessons covered in the earlier chapters. Build these basic principles and mindsets first before emphasizing habits like budgeting and tracking as covered in the next two chapters.

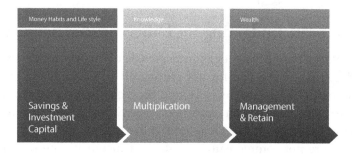

The Progressive Building of the Money Quotient into Our Children:

- Establish the right money habits and lifestyle
- Teach and Train with the right knowledge skills to multiply their capital and savings
- Plan Strategies on how to manage and retain their wealth once they achieve it

To do all these things, they need to know how to live a wealth multiplier lifestyle. We need to teach our children to be clear on their lifestyle first, before moving on to create a budget.

Characteristics of a Wealth Multiplier Lifestyle

Here are the characteristics of a wealth Multiplier Lifestyle and what someone with this lifestyle is concerned with:

1. Acquires Appreciating Assets

Those with a Wealth Multiplier Lifestyle use their money for wealth generating assets instead of only wealth consuming items.

Our children have to be trained and set on course to use the majority of their money for wealth generating assets instead of using their money to reward their emotional impulses and wants. By getting to this place where they understand the value of money and the value of what their money can do for them, they will be less likely to spend it on things that are emotionally driven.

There are basically two types of things you can spend your money on: Appreciating assets and Depreciating assets.

Appreciating assets are things you buy that can go up in value.

These Include:

- Houses

- Land

- Shares

- Collectibles (antiques, watches, pens, comics, toys – things that increase in value over time that you run as a business to sell)

Depreciating assets are basically things that use up your money, which might give you an emotional high, yet do not add any financial value to your life.

These Include:

- Fashionable clothes

- Luxury items, perfumes, cigars

- Expensive holidays

- Expensive jewelry

- Cars and other items that lose value over time

As we teach our children to spend money on appreciating assets, not depreciating assets, they will spend less overall and have more money for investment.

2. Retains Earnings

Those with a Wealth Multiplier Lifestyle Knows how to retain money once they have earned it.

My favorite football club is a club called 'Manchester United'. Their previous manager, who was to retire, managed his last game at their home stadium, Old Trafford. During that game, his team scored five goals, it was fantastic, however they also allowed their competitors five goals.

If we play great offence but have a lousy defense, we still don't win. The same principle applies to our finance. We can be great at going out and making money, but if we do not know how to retain it so we can multiply it, we are going to lose the game as well.

Play good offence and defense. What I mean by this is to attack the economic system to plunder wealth for yourself and your cause, but then also learn good defense, which is how to hold on to your hard earned wealth. There are many people who became millionaires by winning the lottery, but then lost all their wealth within two or three years. Why? Because their win was only a temporary win without the education of how to hold on to their wealth.

It can be very frustrating to see all your hard earned money disappear because of the lack of skills to hold on to it. Teaching our children how to hold on to their wealth will be one of the most valuable lessons you can teach them in life.

The key to this is lifestyle. If they desire a lifestyle they cannot afford, as most people do, they will end up always being in debt and will squander their hard earned wealth.

3. Accumulates Capital for Multiplication

Those with a Wealth Multiplier Lifestyle set a lifestyle for themselves that allows the majority of their money to be used for multiplication instead of exhausting their capital.

My wife's cousin married a plumber in Australia, and when I met him at a family Chinese New Year reunion dinner, I was so impressed when he shared with me how he managed his finances. He owned four houses, and three of them were in well-to-do neighborhoods with excellent infrastructure. Each of these three houses looked great, were well designed and had great amenities. He stayed in the fourth house.

The fourth house had one bathroom, which was shared among the whole family, it was the smallest, and least attractive house. This guy knew how to play good offence and defense. No wonder there are so many plumbers who are millionaires in Australia. Teach your children good offense, but even more importantly make sure they understand great financial defense. If they are not pressured to show off or live a lifestyle to impress anyone, they will hold on to their wealth which will enable them to multiply it.

4. Lives a Life of Contentment

I heard this saying a few times. *"Some people who use money they don't have, to buy the things they cannot afford to impress the people they don't like."*

Many people live to impress others and to keep up with others. This character trait forms at an early age. When our children keep comparing themselves and what they own or where they are to others, we have to check it and deal with it.

Contentment with what we have is an important principle when paired with a drive to be better and to achieve more. A balance is needed. Too much contentment and we can become lazy and unproductive. Too little and we can strive and strive and expend all our energy to impress others yet still never be happy or satisfied with anything in our lives.

What we need is contentment with righteousness. Basically contentment in the right areas, such as family, wife, car, house, and what we have, tempered with a drive to be a better person, to impact more people and to influence others in a positive way. Working to better your life is okay, but at every point in the drive to be better, our children and ourselves need to learn to be content, happy, and satisfied with what we have and where we are while we are working towards being better.

This will enable us to avoid spending money on things we don't need and cannot afford, to impress people we don't like, with money we don't have.

5. Allocates Money to Give to Others

Those with a Wealth Multiplier Lifestyle allocate money within their budget to bless others.

We have already covered the principles of tithing and using our money to bless others. So we know that people who do this regularly become wealthy because money does not have a hold on them.

If we are tightfisted and refuse to bless anyone but ourselves, then we are a miserly person, and chances are our children will hate our lifestyle and later live the opposite, a life of extravagance without boundaries.

I am not saying we should give all our money away, that is also another extreme that is silly, but we should give away a budgeted portion to support a charity or a social cause of our choice.

As discussed earlier, finding a cause for yourself and your children to support is very important in the upbringing of your children.

If our children see that we are living a simple life and saving our money to bless them with a good education or to support a worthy cause, they will emulate the life we live and pick a cause of their own. When we incorporate this principle into our lifestyle our children will plan to use a portion of their money to bless others because they have seen the model in us.

This will attract wealth, friends, a good testimony in society and a joyful life. A life lived well is one that is lived, not just for itself, but for blessing others through the giving of joy, money, time and knowledge.

6. Ruthless About Living Within a Budget

A wealth multiplier lifestyle also ensures that they stick to a budget. We need to teach our children that the first budget does not always reflect our true lifestyle or expenditure. Most people will be unrealistic and set goals they cannot achieve by either leaving out important aspects of their expenditure or trying to cut everything (some important things for them as well).

There are times when drastic cuts are needed and tough decisions need to be made. There are also other times when gradual adjustment and careful planning gives us a realistic chance of achieving a budget. Keep adjusting and cutting down lifestyle choices to get to a point where you live within a budget and teach your children to continue being ruthless on unnecessary spending in order to achieve wealth.

We will cover tracking in the next chapter, which is a major tool for a wealth multiplier, however, I would say at this point that lifestyle choices play the biggest part in whether a budget is achieved or not.

Because most people live a life that is beyond their means and desire this kind of lifestyle, they never achieve wealth. People who do are ruthless with the way they stick to their financial plan. No Extras mean NO EXTRAs and they will work towards achieving this by totally reorganizing their lifestyle and even cut away friends that are not enablers of this lifestyle and who refuse to help or encourage them in their endeavor. They also cut the little things that add up to a big sum that nullifies their financial plan.

7. Focused on Financial Goals

Those with a Wealth Multiplier Lifestyle keep focused on financial goals and are not easily swayed by emotional desires.

One of the key things about wealth multipliers are; they know how to manage their emotions when it comes to desires that can derail them from their financial goals.

Most are familiar with that famous saying, *"Money is the root of all evil."* As it happens, this is really a proverb from the Bible that is often misquoted. The actual verse states, *"… the love of money is the root of all kinds of evil."*

Can you see how this changes the entire connotation and perception of wealth portrayed by this saying? It is not money that is the *root of all evil*, it is the *love* of money. This is an emotional problem. The problem lies in our emotional approach to money and wealth.

If we have an unhealthy desire for money it can supplants everything that is important in our life – our spirituality and connection to God, our family, our friends, our cause and our work. In order to obtain money, we begin to compromise our principles and live in greed. Our emotions become distorted and cause problems for ourselves and others close to us.

That same proverb goes on to add, *"some by longing for it have wandered away from the faith and pierced themselves with many griefs."*

Again we can see that at the core it is an emotional issue. Loving money more than anything else, fearing money, having the mindset of poverty that we do not have enough of it, the desires that come with money, all these things are emotions that can cause us to lose control of our finances. Once we lose control, we lose the ability to achieve our financial goals.

Staying on Track with Your Budget

A common question is, "How do you stay on budget?" Here is how:

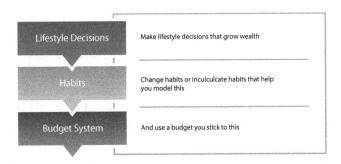

There are three areas to look at to stay on track with a budget. We need to practice it ourselves and teach it to our children.

Choice of Lifestyle

What you choose as a lifestyle and the daily decisions that come with that choice.

Money Habits and Thoughts

What you think about money and what causes you to spend it.

Budgeting System for Management

A budgeting system with proper breakdowns of management of your money and wealth.

Let's look at each of the three in detail:

1. Choice of Lifestyle

Our choice of lifestyle, and it is a choice, is one of the key areas that can allow us, or our children, to achieve wealth faster than you would expect. Lifestyle choices basically make or break our ability to achieve our financial plan and wealth goals. These choices are directly linked to the concepts of Delayed Gratification and Emotions and Money, that I talked about in the first chapter of this book.

Most people choose lifestyles that are beyond their means and are governed solely by emotions without clear boundaries in their management of money. What do I mean by this? They do not model accurate financial principles and are sold on living a consumer lifestyle that is beyond them. Outlined below are a few typical negative financial behavior and thinking patterns. Teach your children to avoid these bad behavior patterns with money by not behaving the same way ourselves.

People who have bad behavior patterns with money:

a. Make choices to reward themselves with depreciating assets with money they could save or use for appreciating assets.

Basically, they use their money only for pleasure rather than making their money work for them. They could have bought properties, shares, unit trusts, made investments on things that would work their money, but instead they will be working for money their whole life.

b. Live a lifestyle to fit in with friends, family, society which they cannot afford just to get some form of affirmation.

This means they make choices to buy a certain car, live in certain neighborhoods and make bad judgments with money to impress people and to show that they have money (when really they do not). They are basically a slave to the opinions of others.

c. They give in to impulses, to reward themselves and these impulses add up and derail them from achieving financial goals.

Most of the time we feel that it is okay to spend a little here on this luxury item and then that one and a later one, but all these add up and use up capital we could have used to invest and build wealth.

d. They feel they have earned the right to enjoy life and spend all their money on luxuries.

It is okay to reward yourself with a portion of your money. A budgeted luxury item within the boundaries of what you can afford is okay if you are already financially free, but if all the money you save throughout the year goes towards one holiday at the end of the year, something is wrong with your concept of financial management.

Teaching our children to avoid these destructive lifestyle choices and behaviors can later save their financial lives.

2. Money Habits and Thoughts

If we think about money as a never ending resource that is going to keep coming to us in the future no matter how we spend it, then both we and our children are one step away from financial disaster.

Money is not a renewable resource and we have to teach our children this at an early age. Most children ask for toys and more and more things that they want. We need to be responsible to teach them to curtail those desires.

What are good habits with money?

- Use only a portion of your return on investment (ROI) for luxuries

- Only allow yourself to spend on a depreciating item that you desire when you have earned three times that sum of money from an appreciating asset.

- Allocate money and budget a small portion for holidays, buying personal items you enjoy and luxuries, not spending any more than budgeted once you have used up the allocation (we will talk about allocation ratios below).

- Be ruthless with tracking your expenses. You must know exactly where your money has gone and how much you have spent on any given day. Keeping a proper record of your expenses is a key success factor in the management and acquisition of wealth (We will cover this in detail in the next section).

3. Budgeting System for Management

A budgeting system can be a great tool if used properly and there is proper financial planning to go along with it. What our children need to learn with a budgeting system, (and most adults as well) is that they need to organize and plan with the money they receive every month (or even week) to achieve certain financial goals.

Financial planning is a regular activity, and the budget is the tool to implement that plan. Here are components of a financial plan that our children can learn and master as well.

Components of Financial Planning:

- They need to decide what savings and investments they want to apportion money to every month.

- They need to have clear financial goals that they are working towards.

- They need to have multiple categories of savings, not just one account where money is put into.

- They need to plan their expenses and lifestyle to facilitate the achievement of the set goals.

- They also need to take into account yearly expenditure.

- These include taxes and subscriptions, insurance and car road tax, or other expenses that are not monthly but yearly or twice yearly. They are infrequent but large expenses. Many people get caught when they suddenly have to come up with larger sums of money.

A good budgeting system needs some fundamentals yet remain adaptable enough to change to meet your requirements. We also need to teach our children what makes a good budgeting system.

Criteria for a good budgeting system:

a. Prioritize Capital Accumulation

Our budgeting system must be a system that prioritizes the raising of capital rather than detailing our expenses. There must be categories we save for and we must be making adjustments to build capital for investments. Some important categories include putting money into our capital accumulating account or wealth building account. This is the main account we would use for investment capital. The more money we put in here the wealthier we are going to be. We also need to budget for a buffer if we don't have one yet. In fact, before we put money into a capital account, we need to build the buffer first. Other categories include saving for holidays (the least amount of money needs to go here) and other planned expenses.

b. Shows an Overview of Budget Items

A good budgeting system must give us an overview of everything we can use our money for. Many people use budget systems they get online only to find that they have missed out a category or forgotten something. The more the budgeting system takes into account our own lifestyle, culture and goals for wealth building, the more complete and effective it is going to be. If there are any areas missed out, it becomes an unplanned expenditure. The more we cover every category, the more we can stick to our plan. Remember, our savings determine our achievement of financial goals.

c. Allows Personalization

We must find a budgeting system that allows us to add in categories personalized to our own financial situation. We may have expense categories or even savings categories that are unique to us. My sister was a divorcee and also someone suffering from depression because of the difficult life she faced and choices she had made. Sadly, she recently passed away. She never held a proper job or went out to work, but had custody of her two children. The father of the children decided to abandon them and never paid a cent towards their education, expenses, and probably would never pay for tertiary education at university. My wife and I felt that it was important to set up an account and budget for their education. So we started doing this and took up the responsibility to deal with this unique situation.

Budget Allocations for Building Wealth

It is critical to organize and apportion our finances and expenses into a budget so that we have a clear plan to follow towards building wealth.

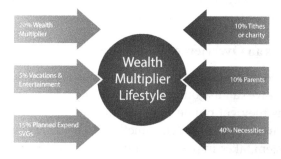

In the above diagram, I have shown the allocation of how ideally our money should be apportioned. Following these principles will allow us and our children to build wealth faster than most other people. It also helps us to plan and organize our finances towards the achievement of our financial goals. More importantly, it will allow us to decide on the kind of lifestyle we want to live to achieve our goals. This principle is based on the Roman money-bags system developed around 2, 000 years ago.

In those times, the Romans use to apportion their money in different bags for different purposes. An off-shoot of this system was used in recent times called the envelope system, where people used to take their paycheck and apportion it for different purposes into envelopes. In fact, my dad used to do this with his salary for many years.

Now with the advent of cashless transactions and credit cards, people become less likely to take out their whole paycheck in cash, however, the system is still useful in a cashless environment. Open up four accounts to apportion your paycheck and money for each of these categories according to the percentages given above:

- Wealth Multiplier
- Planned Expenditure
- Necessities
- Entertainment and Vacations

Each of these categories requires a separate account to save money in. The other two categories mentioned, tithes and parents, can be paid immediately when you receive money and therefore do not require any accounts.

Let me go through this with you step by step.

1. Tithes or Charity – 10%

This is the most important category. If we are sowing into the lives of others as a principle, or are giving back 10% to our spiritual storehouse as a person of faith, then we are going to attract blessings. No matter how difficult your financial situation, practice this and you will not only manage, but will thrive financially in a matter of months. We have already covered this in detail under Principles of Wealth in a previous chapter. I have lost count of how many times we have seen people who were struggling with finance, when they applied this principle began to breakthrough financially. You can refer back to the chapter on Principles of Wealth if you want to revisit this in detail.

2. Wealth Multiplier – 20%

This is a key category if we want to live a wealth multiplying lifestyle. This category includes all our investments, capital for investments, as well as the Return on Investment (ROI) from those specific investments. The more money we give towards our investment capital to grow our wealth, the faster our wealth is going to grow. The key is to cut down from other categories and live a lifestyle that is a wealth multiplier lifestyle.

What do we do with the money in this account? Simply put, we keep adding money to it. Once the money in this account reaches a sufficient amount for us to make an investment, we can use it all for one or several investments. We then repeat the process again with other investment funds.

When selling an investment, the rule I recommend is that you only use 25% of the return to buy something that you need, a better or larger house, or a car if we don't have one (not the most expensive car, but a car that we need). Again, use only 25% of the return on investment. This means that 100% of the capital along with the remaining 75% of the return on investment should be put back into this account. We then wait for the next investment opportunity we can use the money for.

As we keep doing this our money and our investments increase and are paid in full. The amount of assets and cash we now have begin to grow exponentially. It is this account that makes us wealthy. This is our wealth multiplier account.

Some people have asked me what to do with it once it accumulates to millions and they are already in their older years (maybe 70 or more).

- Do they spend it all in one joy-filled shopping experience?

- Do they give it all to their children for them to spend?

- Do they give everything to charity?

The choice is ultimately yours, however, what about building a dynasty of wealth for our children or for our ensuing generations? I would say this is an idea worth considering and one we need to share with our children. Let me explain what I mean. Let's say through working the right investments and the study of proper investments, we invest well and we have achieved all our financial goals. I suggest we enjoy 25% of our ROI, never touching our accumulated capital or 75% of the return on any given investment. Then, let's say both ourselves and our children practice all the principles we have taught them so that at the end of their life at sixty or seventy years of age they have accumulated $ 3, 000, 000 in wealth. This would be my suggestion as to what to do with it:

Put the $3, 000, 000 in a trust account with a bank or an institution that is going to have continuity. Name your posterity (next generation) as beneficiaries. Instruct the trustee to keep making safe investments and to expect and exit these investments after a fixed return, let's say 20% or more if it is property. Keep accumulating the wealth and give (pay out) 50% of the ROI to your posterity. Keep the capital and 50% of the ROI to be put back into the fund, keep doing this over and over again to perpetually grow the fund.

In this manner we can build wealth corporately for our ensuing generations. We can create a business or financial mini empire that could resource the next generation for years to come.

Think about the possibilities. What would happen if this account keeps multiplying over 100 years? We could create wealth for our children and a trust fund to empower our posterity for generations to come.

3. Planned Expenditure Savings – 15%

This is the savings category for short-term savings towards a predefined purpose. Such planned expenditures could be the purchase of a car, a down payment for the house we are to live in, education for our children or other short-term and slightly longer-term purchase decisions or expenditures we are going to need to use money for.

15% looks like very little, however we can reduce our expenditure from our necessities column to add percentage points to this category. Never reduce amounts from the tithes and charity or giving to parents. Also as a rule, never reduce any percentage from your wealth multiplier account. You will need to spend money on transport (a car), housing, and education for your children, so it is good to have a category planned that includes all these needed expenses (but don't put luxuries in this category).

4. Vacations and Entertainment – 5%

I believe this is the least important category and we can have even less of a percentage here if others are more needed. We talked a lot in the first two chapters about delayed gratification and finding ways to unwind without spending money, things such as going for a walk, enjoying a hobby like cycling, or playing with our children to unwind. If we need a holiday, why not visit a family member or someone we know who enjoys our company and let them do the same with us. This saves on hotels and other unnecessary expenditure. Why not consider going for local holidays instead of holidays abroad?

If this is really important to us, and our finances are in order, and we want to have a holiday and can afford it, go ahead, but no more than 5% of our income should go towards this.

It is important to regularly take breaks and enjoy life with our children, however, we should keep our financial goals as a priority in our mind. If our holiday is going to be a setback in our financial future and we are going to take money from our wealth multiplier account, then I think we have to realize ourselves and also teach our children that it is just not worth doing it. We should never sacrifice our future on the altar of the now.

5. Parents – 10%

I had a huge difficulty convincing people that this is important in welfare states. Some people feel it is the government's responsibility to take care of their parents and not their own responsibility. This is a life principle. If we provide for our parents (the ones that provided for us) we attract wealth. I have covered this in detail earlier under the Principles of Wealth.

In short, the way we teach our children to honor their parents is by modeling the right behavior for them by honoring ours. A lot of people say that their parents were not good parents, and that they did not provide for them well or made a lot of mistakes. Parents will have to answer for what they have done, regardless you and I still have to honor our parents. Honor has nothing to do with how our parents have treated us. Honor is a principle to be practiced irrespective of what they did or did not do. There are exceptions however, such as if your parent sexually abused you, and has not changed, then do not support them. If they are mentally unstable, create a fund for them and get them expert care.

6. Necessities – 40%

This is where we will notice the biggest chunk of our expenses going towards, therefore, we have to do a proper budget. Decide on a lifestyle that reflects your goals then set your budget accordingly. If any of us, including our children want to be millionaires, the majority of our money needs to be going towards our wealth multiplier account.

Our needs can be cut down to basics, but many people confuse needs with wants and wants are luxuries. Let me give you an example - Do you need a car to go to work or a BMW? If you can afford a BMW by all means go for it, but many consider it a necessity to impress their clients and friends. Let me be clear; IT IS NOT A NECCESITY IT IS A LUXURY!

I recommend that no more than 40% of our money should go to covering all our living expenses. This should include housing, transport, fuel, food, groceries, utilities and phone bills. There might be other expense categories, but really check if you need them, and if you don't, make sure that you cut them away.

A mistake that many people make is that when they earn $ 3, 000 they live like they earn $ 3, 000, and when their income goes up to $ 10, 000 a month, they live like they earn $ 10, 000. They never have enough to build wealth. The secret is to live like we earn $ 3, 000 when we earn $ 10, 000.

This is our leakage account, when we have more expenses than money to spend, we will never get wealthy. The key to reducing expenses is choosing our lifestyle. Making sure we teach our children not to get caught up in a lifestyle that does not multiply wealth is paramount.

I once had someone who kept borrowing money from me because she claimed that she didn't have enough. When I asked if she was living a basic lifestyle she claimed she was. One day, I had enough, and I told her that if she wanted to borrow any more money she had to sit down with me and work through her expenses. She was reluctant at first, but because she wanted to borrow money she eventually agreed.

When I went through her expense categories of every month, there were bills like $ 60 for a haircut at a high-end salon, and $ 200 for her one and only dog because of high-end, high-priced dog food. There were other luxury expenses as well, but when I suggested that she cut down and go to a cheaper place to cut her hair, buy cheaper dog food, or even to prepare her own food for her dog, she got upset and refused to change.

Many people simply do not want to change their lifestyle, which prevents them from living within their means. This, in turn, sabotages their ability to gain wealth, and ensures that they never achieve their financial goals.

We must be responsible to teach our children differently, getting them to live an accurate lifestyle and cutting expenses down to real necessities only.

Troubleshooting the Budget Allocation

What happens if you are having difficulties with making the categories and allocations work for your current situation?

When starting out if you or your child cannot live within the amounts and percentages I have recommended for these categories, this example shows what you can do:

- Keep your expenses as low as possible, and calculate what percentage of your income your total expenses amount to.

- We must never compromise on Tithes and Charity, because this is what opens the gates of blessings and increase into our lives.

- You have calculated your expenses (inclusive of tithes) and they still come up to 80% of your total income.

- This leaves a balance of 20% of your total income to allocate to the remaining categories.

- Apportion this 20% budget balance into the same categories as mentioned above, however, using the following recommended percentages applied to the 20% budget balance amount.

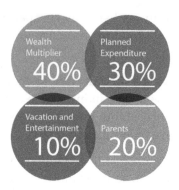

- These percentages can be applied to any percentage of balance left over in the budget after your expenses and tithes have been deducted.

- If it is not practical for you to follow these new ratios, then you can also adjust the ratios to suit your own situation.

- Keep the Wealth Multiplier and the Planned Expenses accounts as the biggest portions if you adjust the ratios.

- Remember, the purpose of our budget is to set and follow a plan that will enable capital accumulation and wealth building.

Start practicing with what you have and where you are in your current situation. Then move on forward by gradually increasing the amounts saved and reducing the expenditure.

You can also use the budget template given below to work out your budget and savings. Feel free to customize it to suit your own financial plan, but keep to the principles of a Wealth Multiplier Lifestyle.

A Budget Template

Income	$
Salary	
Spouse	
Business Income	
Dividends	
Rental	
Total	0

Savings	$
Wealth Multi.	
Short Term	
House Fund	
Childs Education	
Total	0

Investments	$
Unit Trust	
Share Market	
Property	
Land	
Total	0

Insurance	$
Total	0

Household Expense	$
Rental	
Car	
Satellite	
Phones	
Electricity	
Groceries	
Food	
Newspapers	
Petrol	
Health	
Total Household Ex	0
Total Expenses	

Debt Repay	$
TOTAL DB	0

Annual Payments	0

Tithe & Off	$
Total	0
Parents	$
Total	0

Fun	$
Holidays	
Entertainment	
Eating Out	
Total	0
Annual	$
Tax	
Subscriptions	
Total	0

Savings & Investment	

Surplus	0

EXERCISE: Setting a Budget
Planning and Living for Wealth Acquisition

For Ages 5-8

1. Work out a budget for your child to spend pocket money at school everyday, it could be a dollar a day or less depending on your own country and its cost of goods and services

2. Give your child slightly more than the budget (30-50% more) and tell them this is for them to save and use at the end of the week for a special treat

3. The treat can either be an ice cream, pancakes or a healthy snack which they like at the end of the week. The key is they must like it

4. The money they save everyday must amount to a sum just enough for the treat at the end of the week

5. If they overspend one day in the week, they cannot afford the treat

6. After doing this exercise for a period, teach them the power of budgeting and keeping on track. You need to share with them what you practice and how you budget to keep the family expenses on track

7. You can repeat the exercises I shared in the first chapter about the toy and saving up for it

For Ages 9-12

1. Repeat the exercise in the first chapter and get the child to save every week to earn enough to buy a toy

2. Also sit down with your child and explain the concept of budgeting and show them how you budget, step by step. Do not rush

3. Do not worry if your child does not understand everything you are saying and only some parts sink in. They are catching the concepts

For Ages 13-17

Part 1

1. Take the time to sit down with your child and explain how you budget for a year or monthly. Show them all the expenses and how you manage them

2. Show your child how much you are saving for their education as well

3. Most parents keep this from their child and this does not enable or empower the child to learn that they have to be careful with money

Part 2

1. Work out a monthly budget for your child in terms of their pocket money, transport, clothing, movies and entertainment, hanging out with friends and other basic expenditures that your adolescent would use money for

2. Work out how much they are going to spend on it every year

3. Sit down with your child and work out a budget with them so they understand the process

4. Give them the money monthly and get them to write down all their expenses

5. If they overspend, they cannot use money for entertainment or things they like. Alternatively, you can deduct money from the next month if they overspend on entertainment one month for example

6. Don't compromise on health if they finish their lunch or break money for food, get them to take food from the house

7. The key is that you work with your child every week for the first few weeks or months to keep them on track and teach them how to budget and manage their money, they will keep the right habits even when they leave home to work or go to university

Chapter 6

Expense Tracking
Tracking Every Dollar to Achieve Financial Goals

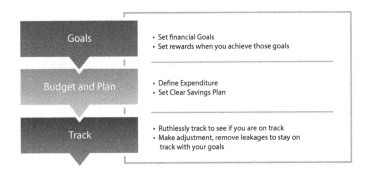

Goals	• Set financial Goals • Set rewards when you achieve those goals
Budget and Plan	• Define Expenditure • Set Clear Savings Plan
Track	• Ruthlessly track to see if you are on track • Make adjustment, remove leakages to stay on track with your goals

It is not enough just to have a budget or different budgets for accountability. It is more important for us to have a system that allows us to manage our budget implementation daily in order to see whether we are on track. Many people come up with budgets, and just as many cannot stick to them. Why? Because they do not track their expenses and progressively monitor whether they are on budget.

This is one of the most important principles we can teach our children. It is linked very much to the principle of accountability I mentioned earlier, however, this is so important I wanted to write about it as a principle of its own.

When trying to lose weight, people who check their weight every day, are more successful than those who do not. Why? It's simple accountability. People who know they are going to weigh themselves, and who have a habit of doing so regularly, will be more careful with their eating habits and therefore will not eat junk. They are also less prone to eating-binges, which upset the careful tracking of their weight.

One of the biggest keys to financial success is tracking our expenses. This absolutely must be taught to our children. If we have a proper tracking system and we track our expenses regularly, we will be less likely to splurge. It is the same principle as with the weight loss.

Successful business people do not just keep an eye on their sales, they also track their expenses. It would be a disaster for the business if they didn't. A business can keep getting money in, but if they do not manage it and monitor the expenses and costs, the profit margin can be eaten up so quickly that they can be out of business in just a matter of months.

On my website www.raymondgabriel.com I posted an expense tracking system for people who need one to be able to use it. It is copyrighted though, so you cannot re-sell it. It is posted there for you or your benefit to download and put it to work towards building wealth.

It is a simple tracking system created in an Excel spreadsheet document. It allows you to track your (or your children's) expenses with preset categories. This is important because it is not just a matter of writing every cent down as we spend it, but it is about writing it down in a way that is systematic and easy to understand. Your tracking system must be one that is simple, easy to use, and pleasant. It has to be one that works for you. It must be something that you enjoy doing every day otherwise you and your children will not get into the habit of tracking your expenses. Managing your finances daily helps you to achieve your goals, because you can identify problem areas and make adjustments day to day and not wait until it is too late.

Characteristics of a Good Tracking System

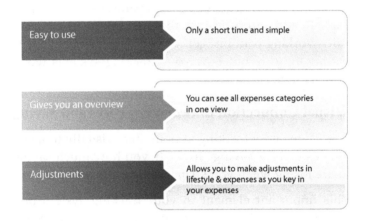

Easy to use	Only a short time and simple
Gives you an overview	You can see all expenses categories in one view
Adjustments	Allows you to make adjustments in lifestyle & expenses as you key in your expenses

1. Gives an At-a-Glance Overview of Expenditure

A good expense tracking system must give you an overview of your financial situation daily in one glance.

Before I developed the system posted on my blog, I tried using various financial tracking systems and I always found many of them (although there are some good ones) had one flaw. They looked great design-wise, but were very complicated to use and made you key in multiple things before you could use them. The system I developed has just one simple entry and is easy to fill in. More importantly you can see all expense categories in one simple layout. Which is very important because you need to have an overview of your finances. You need to be spending time and energy getting an overview of where you are financially every day. This shows what steps you need to take to mitigate situations where you are going out of the plan.

2. Uncomplicated Item Entry

A good expense tracking system will allow you to put in entries easily without complication.

Having predefined categories and places for entry linked to days in a month is another very important factor. When you or your children are using a tracking system, you must be able to add entries fast, so that you can focus on strategically working your budgets or your expenses, not spending time figuring out how your tracking systems works, and what items go where.

3. Visual Connection Between Expenses and Savings

A good expense tracking system must visually link your expenses to your savings to show you how much savings you are losing when you keep having outflows of money.

This important element in your tracking system must show the link between lowered expenses and increased savings (as I have covered above). You must know on a monthly basis, where you are in terms of your monthly expenses, savings, and where you are in terms of strategic planning to save every month to achieve your financial goals. The best financial tracking systems link expenses to a monthly savings system.

4. Relevant Expense Categories

A good expense tracking system must have categories of expenses that make sense for you and your financial situation.

When I designed my tracking system, I thought about

expense categories rather than simply a system to record every expense in a disorganized way. Expense categories help you classify your expenses being tracked and calculations into easily understood columns. I used around 10-12 categories depending on what was relevant to the group I was training with the tracking system. For example, students have very different categories to working adults or business people, however every group must understand the fundamentals of tracking and how to use every column.

5. Customizable to Individual Requirements

A good expense tracking system must be customizable to suit your particular individual requirements.

A participant of one of my trainings had a lot of friends and was spending money on birthdays and gifts for her friends very regularly. She customized my system and added a category for gifts. Feel free to customize the system I developed because for it to work for you it must suit your own requirements. However, do bear in mind that if you can add your expense into a ready category, it may not be exactly the category that suits you, but it does have relevance. A category must be an area in your tracking system where you add in expenses regularly, that is, more than just once or twice a month. If you are only giving out gifts once a month you can put it under the miscellaneous category.

6. Accounts for Total Income

A good expense tracking system must account for all the income you earn as well as all the expenses you spend money on.

I even write down claimable items like air travel and hotels, which my company pays for as I represent it for training. When you get your claims refunded you can add them to your income column. It must also include all sources of household income; share dividends (unless you are reinvesting 100% of the ROI back into another investment, following my advice on capital building), business, spouse's salary, property rental etc. This system must be complete as an overview so that you do not have a complicated system that has multiple areas for the different categories or that relies entries from different places that you cannot view at a glance. You need to see everything as an overview so that you can make adjustments as things or circumstances change.

7. Ease of Use

A good expense tracking system must be easy to use.

There is no point in having a complicated tracking system where you have to make multiple entries to key in one expense item. You have to first pick the most suited category where the expense is to be located, key in or pick the type of expense, pick a graphic or icon so it can be seen, add the date, and three other things for it to work. Complication is not always better.

A good expense tracking system must be able to track all your expenses for you, your wife, and your children in no more than five minutes a day at the end of each day. The easier a system is to use, the more you are going to use it.

A Simple Expense Tracking System

Listed on the next page is a simple tracking system that is subdivided into categories. At the end of each day when you come home, record the total amount you have spent for the entire day. For example on the 2nd of the month your breakfast lunch and dinner amounted to $ 40 so you would add that amount in on the 2nd under food, and so on.

Date	Food	Petrol /Transport	Toll & Parking	Personal Items	Groceries	Leisure	Monthly Payments	Misc / Savings
1								
2								
3								
4								
5								
6								
7								
8								
9								
10								
11								
12								
13								
14								
15								
16								
17								
18								
19								
20								
21								
22								
23								
24								
25								
26								
27								
28								
29								
30								
31								

If you have a spouse both of you could do it together at the end of the day. There is an automated version in excel format on my blog that auto calculate the totals for you.

Results of Effective Expense Tracking

Good things start to happen when you track your expenses. It begins to put you in the driver's seat of your own financial future.

1. Capital for Investment

Some times when I look at a financial course that is being advertised I see some similarities. There is always a promise of getting rich quick. *"How to become a millionaire in 1 year! How I took $ 20, 000 and turned it into $ 200, 000 in three months. Ten steps to turn $ 100, 000 into $ 1 Million."* There are so many promises of quick and easy wealth.

While some of these techniques may work, for every one of them there is a pre-requisite, you need capital. In all my years of educating parents and their children on finance, I have found that many adults are struggling with basic financial foundations. The parents themselves lack a decent Money Quotient, yet they want to know about tips for the stock market or quick steps to become rich. Most of these adults do not even have any capital to invest. They have been living a life without financial principles. Yet they are going for courses that talk about turning $ 100, 000 to $ 1, 000, 000.

Simply put, we need to teach our children, there are no quick steps, there are only foundations to lay and build upon when it comes to money. If we practice and build on the foundations, we get wealthy. Tracking is one of the best and fastest ways to raise the capital we need to make investments. If we make the right investments consistently and reinvest our returns we will get wealthy. It is an inevitable result of a life lived by principles.

2. Staying On Budget

I know many people who have done budgets, sat down, planned everything and then got frustrated because they do not seem to be sticking to the budget. All their effort seems to be in vain. Developing a budget is not enough, we have to stay on track. The key here is not for us to have a plan, it is adjusting every day to stay on it. When we do a budget, there will definitely be things that suddenly turn up that we have to pay for, and this will throw us off our budget. What a tracking system allows us to do is to get back on alignment. This is a key principle we need to teach our children. There is no point teaching them how to budget without teaching them how to track their expenses.

Let's say your budget is $ 500 for eating out every month, this works out to $ 25 a day (taking just working days and not weekends for example). Then let's say a common thing happens... there is a night out with friends and you go out and spend a little more that the budget allows. Is the budget ruined? No, it is not, it is just out of alignment. You just need to bring it back into alignment. So let's say on that particular night out, you spend $ 100. That is, four days' worth of your food budget. Since you are tracking your expenses you can spot this early and make adjustments for the rest of the month accordingly. You could change it so you eat out at $ 15 a day so you meet the budgetary requirement at the end of the month. What happens if the expenditure is at the end of the month and you have no time to recover? Well, then you can cut down the following month.

The key here is to teach our children to live according to their budget and to make adjustments so that they don't get frustrated with little things that go out of whack. They can always recuperate. What a tracking system does is it allows us to spot things early, to make adjustments and to stay on track.

Once we get this going we will be able to go to the next step, which is working and planning our expenses annually.

3. Increased Financial Confidence

Your financial confidence increases because you are managing well and are on top of the state of your financial affairs.

Imagine if our children or even ourselves starts our first coaching session on soccer. We have to learn how to kick the ball, how to pass the ball, how to run, and where to run when we are offside, and so many other things. . There seems to be so much to learn, but as we come from each coaching session and practice session thereafter, confidence increases, and we start doing things with the ball that we have never done before.

Financial management is the same. At first it seems as if there is so much to learn and pick up and we wonder if we will 'get it.' Investments, trading, technical analysis, fundamental analysis... it might seem very new to us and our children, but as we keep learning more and more, we gain more confidence and pick up more techniques and knowledge that becomes useful to us, both as a parent who is teaching as well as our children are learning.

Tracking improves our confidence tremendously because it now seems as if we are doing the right thing and working through our money like a professional money manager. We have a plan, and we are in control of that plan. We know what goes where and how much we have at any given time. We know where our money is going and what we have used it for at any point in time. This gives us and our children huge confidence and the ability to build wealth faster.

Confidence always improves greatly when we know that we are doing the right things. It seems as if our life and our children's lives are coming into order. Indeed we will even have people asking our children for advice, (especially among their friends). People gravitate towards those who are role models and leaders in their field and tracking expenses definitely makes our children role models who will be able to impact and influence others around them.

4. Achievement of Financial Goals

You achieve your financial goals and dreams because a financial tracking system helps you to live towards your goals on a daily basis.

When our children set strong financial goals, like for example to be debt free by twenty eight years of age or to own their first property by twenty-five years of age, they have to make adjustments and continuously realign their spending habits and other habits to keep them in the running for those goals. This is one of the most important principles we can teach our children and it is applicable in every field. Imagine if your child wants to be an Olympic sprinter. They will have to start early, eat right for every day of their lives, and they will have to train rigorously daily to keep pushing themselves up to higher levels, never just being content to be where they are. This is because to become an Olympic sprinter they have to qualify with the right times, to qualify they have to train and subject their body to a rigorous routine. Then the day finally comes when they reach the qualifying stage and they are at the starting position ready to run the race to qualify for the Olympics and represent their country. That starting position was not their starting point, it was a culmination of maybe ten years of living, doing specific things every day, from diet to training regimes to get to that point.

People who achieve their goals need to be living daily to achieve those goals. This holds true for financial goals as well. This is what I mean when talking about our children having the goals I mentioned such as to own their first property at twenty-five years of age. They are boundary breakers, they have to live every day with discipline, track every expense, work out and implement budgets that allow them to achieve these goals, which normally takes an ordinary person much longer to achieve. Acquiring a high Money Quotient as being taught here allows them to achieve it faster.

When some days or even weeks are off-budget, by following a strict and proper financial tracking system, and making adjustments to their expenses the following week or weeks, they are more likely to be financial high achievers who reach their financial goals sooner than most others.

Troubleshooting When Off-Budget

What to do when you track your expenses and are off-budget? To solve any problem you have to first identify the root cause. Determine the cause of the problem and employ a strategy that will adequately address it. Then take action and got to work on the strategy.

Work through these steps and strategies to troubleshoot when going off-budget:

1. Identify the Cause

It could be a lifestyle issue, it is more often than not.

Many adults confuse needs for wants. They feel luxury items, like a new handbag or new shirt, are things they really need. They give themselves excuses, they say that they just got a promotion and need to look the part, that their social status has changed and they need a $1, 000 dollar bag to show people their new status. However, they are doing this without realizing that true millionaires do not really have the need to get expensive bags to impress people.

Some people feel they need a fancy car to impress clients or else they won't get the business they desire or impress the client enough to get a contract. Such deep-seated desires are basically humans with emotional triggers of joy that come from luxury items, wants and desires. Their minds tell them that they need those things, but they are basically wants. People with strong personalities and great powers of persuasion sometimes convince themselves that the lifestyle they cannot afford is something that they need, that it is necessary and not just something they want.

In a child these types of desires are formed by some sort of lack in their lives and need for validation. They are compensating for this lack with material things.

This is why Chapters One and Two are of great importance. We need to avoid having our emotions mess up our financial plan. Most people, children included, are driven by emotions. The key is to manage them and exercise control, not letting our emotions control us. Our children need to be taught this at a very early age. They need to learn that giving in to wrong emotions has bad consequences for them and it is not tolerated. This enables them to understand boundaries, and allows them to find better ways to express themselves.

Impulse buying is one of the main reasons people do not achieve financial goals. To control impulse buying, people need to understand how to be brutal about their needs and wants. It also helps if our mindset is set on appreciating assets instead of depreciating assets. The right mindset is one of the most important things for ourselves and our children to cultivate with regards to using money. If the majority of our money is being used for appreciating assets, instead of depreciating assets, our mindset and our children's mindsets, are in the right place. This too can become addictive like a game. Start your children investing with you early.

They can:

- Invest with you by giving a small portion towards a property you are buying. You should do a contract with them to show them what percentage of the property they own. Make the experience as true to life and serious as possible.

- They can buy shares by pooling their money with you, provided you understand the share market. Get them excited by using a mobile app like Bloomberg to track your share increase daily or weekly together with them.

- You can get them to invest in other things you are investing in, such as unit trusts, or alternative investments you might be doing in collectable toys, wine or other things they find interesting. The key is that it is something they understand and show an interest in. Anything is okay, provided you explain risk, and talk them through the consequences.

- Teach them the concept of diversification by getting them to have a mixed basket of investments. Let them invest portions of their money in a few different areas like unit trusts, properties, shares, and other investments as well.

The idea is to get their emotions excited and their minds engaged with the fact that they are making money via their own investments. They will be less likely to be excited about spending money on their wants with the incentive of their own ROI as a tangible result.

This creates a lifestyle that sets them up for wealth in the future.

2. Adjust and Realign

You just need to readjust and realign future expenses to compensate and quickly get back on track.

You have not failed when things go out of budget, especially with situations you cannot control, like medical expenses, emergencies etc. You just need adjustment. When you see that you are off-budget, just take stock and readjust. Take small steps and come back into alignment.

Let me give you an example. Let's say you overspend on a friend's birthday party. You are supposed to be apportioning just $ 30 to eating out every day, however, this night out was unplanned and expenses for the night came up to $ 100, so you have just blown three or more days of your budget in a single outing. Do not despair, the tracking system will allow you to make adjustments.

You can cut down your daily food expenditure to just $ 15 until you make up the extra $ 70 you spent. This approach should take you only five days.

By tracking your expenses daily, you can make adjustments to your expenses to get back on track. This would not likely be possible if you are tracking what you spend once a month or every couple of weeks and this will NEVER happen if you are not tracking anything in the first place. You will go off the rails without even knowing it ever happened. This is the story of most people's financial lives.

3. Catch and Curtail Habitual Pitfalls

Do you have weaknesses and impulse purchases that need to be curtailed?

If you track your expenses regularly, you will be able to see patterns of where you are going out of budget. What are purchases or expenditures that are regularly tripping you or your child up? Children can start using this system as soon as they are given pocket money.

When I first started tracking I was amazed at the amount of money I spent eating out. Even though eating out in Malaysia is cheap, this adds up and creates some expenses that can be avoided if you plan ahead and pack a sandwich or something from home.

There could be other areas as well for example, buying clothes. A little does not contribute significantly to your leak, but this can add up and take up even 10% of your budget. Your child might be going to a video game arcade and spending up to 50% of their pocket money on the machines there. When they track their expense, they might opt to save up their money instead, and buy a game once that they can play again and again at home in order to curtail the expenditures and save money.

Wherever there are impulse purchases, you can avoid them and work on how you are going to eliminate those habits. For example, I always tell people that if they have to buy something every time they go into a shopping center, and they are broke, with high debt, then just avoid shopping centers. Get other people to make necessary purchases for you. Why put yourself in situations where your bad habits are going to trip you up?

Similarly, there are some children who love tech stuff and computers, and just "must have" the latest gadgets. If your child has this problem, teach them to avoid going to tech stores and browsing or window-shopping. Putting themselves in a precarious spending situation only opens the window for them to leak more expenses impulsively. Instead, teach your child to set a goal and save a portion of their money, let's say 5%, towards this goal. When they reach the savings goal and have the money they specially put aside for their tech toys, they can use it and spend it as a planned purchase.

4. Spend Adequate Time

You have to spend the time, frequently analyzing your expenses.

Habits form us, or so the saying goes, and habits also form our financial success. With consistent tracking, as time goes by, you will be able to gain a very good overview of your finances; where you are going wrong and where you are going right. You will be able to plan to reduce or even eliminate certain categories all together.

Instead of eating at the school cafeteria, your children might want to take food from home and reduce this expense altogether.

You may find that you entertain a lot, and instead of going out to various restaurants, you may want to get a country club membership that allows you to entertain at subsidized rates (provided your club rates are lower than restaurants).

Certain countries allow you to claim fuel as a business expense, which reduces or eliminates the category immediately. With the exception of when you are going on personal trips, you can put this expense under your business and claim it (provided you have enough profit to pay yourself and your staff).

Tracking and regularly looking at your expenses allows you to make informed decisions about your finances. It allows you to make necessary adjustments when you go off-budget and also accurate changes to your lifestyle in order to achieve your financial goals.

It's really that easy!

In Summary

Giving your children the basics of budgeting and tracking are the foundations of a sound Money Quotient that allows for a successful financially healthy life. Don't let them give in to the wrong impulses or attitudes as most adults do. Instead, give them an edge by building their Money Quotient.

When your child learns that money is something they have to manage, and not just look at receiving as a paycheck every month or week, they will start to understand that with managing finance there is a bigger picture. This bigger picture entails working with their money to achieve, in their future, something greater and bigger than normally possible for people with their income levels and earning capacity. Once your children grasp this, they will be disciplined with their lifestyle. They will keep organizing and cutting down, or adjusting their expenses to suit their goals. They will be financially free.

Of all the things I have taught in financial courses, I have never seen a single concept cause more people to breakthrough financially than budgeting and tracking. It is a cornerstone financial habit of those with a high Money Quotient.

EXERCISE: Expense Tracking
Tracking Every Dollar to Achieve

For Ages 5-12

1. Give your child daily pocket money or weekly if they can handle it, making sure you give them a bit more than you normally do so that they can use money when they go out with you for other purchases - such as treats and things that you would normally buy for them.

2. Before you give your child any money, give them a weekly goal as to how much you want them to save by the end of the week (or two weeks), and also how much they should save and spend daily.

3. Get your child to write down what they have spent at a fixed time every day with you when they return home.

4. If they have overspent for the day then plan whether your child wants to take less money the following day so that they can reduce what they spend to achieve the weekly goal of the total amount to be saved.

For Ages 13-17

1. First teach your child how to use the tools in this chapter; the tracking and budgeting system.

2. Give your child the responsibility of paying a few small bills for themselves and for the house for a month.

3. Get them to imagine they are earning a small salary and have to use it for their pocket money and also to pay these bills.

4. DO a budget with them and plan for unforeseen expenses.

5. Get them to track ruthlessly (every day for a month) to stay on budget and to pay those bills. You could even drive them to the place where they have to pay it.

6. A month later when this exercise is completed get your child to imagine a normal, average salary of an adult who just started working and get him to work out a budget for it.

Chapter 7

Finance 101
Basic Rules for Multiplying Wealth

The rules of financial multiplication are based on principles of wealth. As long as we don't operate with these principles, we will not breakthrough financially. In the earlier chapters we have talked about principles to manage wealth, and how to hold on to it so that we can multiply it, and use part of it for our family, our life and our cause.

In this chapter, we will look at some basic rules for multiplying wealth that are very important for us to teach our children. However, as stated before, teaching them alone is not enough, they must see us modeling it.

In fact, actively managing and multiplying our money should be our most important business, not our business or job itself. Our children should see us managing our money and our investments as if they are our first and most important business. Multiplication must be the key part of our financial increase and the management of what we multiply. It is the offensive, or the attack part of our wealth management strategy. Retaining our wealth is the defensive part of our wealth management strategy. Our defensive strategy is the main factor that allows us to retain what we have multiplied and increased. Playing a good combination of offense and defense is critical to building our long-term wealth.

Why People Lose Money on Investments

There are many reasons why people lose money. Our children will be very well equipped if they understand the four main reasons why people have lost money in investments.

These are as follows:

Greed

No Research

Herd Mentality

No Time Spent

1. Greed

Greed causes very intelligent people to make very foolish decisions. Greed in an investment context is the desire to make more money faster by any means, even if violating sound financial principles. It is also wanting more without a purpose; wanting more purely for the sake of just having more.

For example, if someone buys a share at $10 and this share goes up to $15 at this point, for some people greed kicks in. Instead of following the rules of investment, where they have established an exit strategy based on a profit goal, they decide to wait, trusting it will go up even more. More often than not, people like this sees the whole market suddenly drop leaving them stuck with a share that is worth $8 when they bought it at $10.

We have to know when to go into the market and when to come out of the market. We cannot operate on with greed, wanting more and more for yourself, without a plan or purpose.

Greed is usually about self and self-pleasure. The opposite of greed is generosity, using our money or giving your money to help others. It is thinking of money as something not just for ourselves, but something that can be used to make a huge difference to individuals and communities around us.

2. Lack of Due Diligence

Many people jump at investing in different instruments with a lack of knowledge and understanding of the subject matter. For example, they might have read a short article about investing in hedge funds and how that can generate large returns. As a result, they jump right in without thinking about the consequences, and also without the proper knowledge of what to look out for before investing and when to go in and when to get out.

The lack of research is one of the main reasons why our children or ourselves could lose money in investments. We must know and teach our children to understand the following about anything we consider investing in. It is what I call basic the research that is needful before each investment for you and your children to be astute investors.

Here are the crucial components of a good investment research plan:

a. How the Investment Works

How we make money with the particular investment, how the investment generates its income and what the system is like, are all things we need to know about any investment we are considering. If we do not understand the system and how to generate income with that particular investment, the chances of us making a mistake quickly becomes higher. Therefore, we will lose more money with that investment than other more knowledgeable investors who do understand how it works and at what price to buy and what price to sell.

b. When are the right times to go in and get out of the investment?

An exit strategy is paramount when we are looking at investments. What price we buy at has a lot to do with when we are buying. Every investment has peak times and low points. It is always better to buy when the investment is at a low period and slowly moving up.

c. How the investment generates income.

This is an important key success factor in investments that we, and our children, must know and understand. How does this investment make money? In the past, I had a group of friends who kept telling me and other friends about an investment in an educational website project. When I went to the presentation where they were trying to sign up more investors in their scheme, I asked how they were generating money to pay back the promised returns. They would deflect my question and not answer. I kept insisting and they became irritated. So I suspected that they were running a bogus scheme.

d. What are the risk factors and what can you lose?

Our children need to understand that no matter the amount of research we do, we can still lose money on any investment. All investments carry risk. They need to know what the factors are that can cause a potential failure with our investment. With investments, what can go wrong will go wrong. Here are some examples of what to consider: Can we wait out a low period? If our investment does not pan out, what will our consequences be? Can we live with losing that sum of money? Will we be able to make it back from elsewhere?

e. What are the cycles and times of investment peaks?

Investments go up and down based on trends, economic climates, and market sentiment. There are also cycles of peaks and lows. If we study a particular investment we are interested in, we should teach our children when would be the right time to go in, and when would be the right time to come out of an investment. Some investments, like shares, also see a peaking of prices, which are basically high at certain times of the year in certain markets. Knowing when to buy a share and when to sell it can even gain us, or our children, a profit in a matter of months if other market conditions are right.

f. How much do they want to make from this investment, and what do people normally make?

This addresses greed and other traits that can cause us to lose money. Decide exactly how much you want to make either in monetary amounts or percentages before you buy a share or put your money into an investment, and then sell it when you make that amount. Many people have lost money because they hold on to an investment too long trying to time a peak just to see it tumbling back down to a low point. There is always a time when every investment will drop after going through some highs.

g. What are their legal rights with the investment?

I always teach people that they must know what their legal rights are, especially with some types of investments. Always read the fine print, and know who owns your investment, you or the bank? This can be seen in the case of Gold certificates vs. physical Gold.

A Gold certificate is an instrument that shows you own that specific form of value from a financial institution, not the actual Gold itself. When you own physical Gold, you can trade or sell it immediately for money to whomever wants to purchase it. A Gold certificate, even one linked to Gold prices is really just an instrument. At a time of a crash, or if the financial institution you buy the certificate from crashes, you might end up owning nothing but paper. Your legal rights through a trustee account vs. a direct ownership could also give you different legal rights. You need to know and understand your legal rights as an investor.

h. They need to know that the organization they are using to buy the investment is legally set up, and they will have recourse if things go wrong.

There have been many cases in my country where investment clubs and investment organizations have been run from internet based organizations. As a result, when people have lost money, they had no recourse. In other cases, organizations go after friends of friends and then disappear because no legal entity was set up and everything was done through word of mouth. Everyone loses money without a legal recourse and good people get themselves into trouble unnecessarily if they do not research their investments.

i. They need to research others who have done the investment and know what the market is saying about that particular investment and whether the sentiment is still current?

There was some excitement amongst people I knew recently about gold based investments with a company claiming to trade in gold for a good return. It sounded suspicious to me. When a close associate of mine asked me to check out the claims of returns and their legitimacy, I just Googled the organization, and queried the banks they claimed to be working with (who happened to be my clients, as I produced a TV show on financial education with them). I found out some amazing things. The directors of the organization in question have had their business shut down in a neighboring country and were being investigated for fraud. Many people in the neighboring country lost a lot of money. We can truly learn from other people's mistakes. Take a balanced view and learn what other people did, or what their viewpoints are on the company you are looking to invest in.

j. They also need to know about up and coming regulations and bylaws and how it will impact the investment.

Some things can have a negative effect on investments. Property gains tax for example, that taxes people who sell their property within a certain period after the property was bought to discourage property price speculations and protect the property market. This type of laws can have an effect on property prices, because people have to hold on to property for longer periods and might be less likely to buy unless it is a really good deal, or if they feel safe holding on for the long term. We must be aware of which regulations may factor into the investment we are considering.

k. They need to understand the economic climate of the country they are investing in.

If there are signs and news that tell you the country is heading for a recession, then you need to hold on to your money and not spend it too quickly. You can multiply your money faster if you work with the economic cycles and have access to cash during a recession. You can also have more options and can take your pick of good investment opportunities at a lower price if you buy things during a recession or have the bargaining power that cash affords at such times.

3. Herd Mentality

People sometimes go into an investment based on a rumor. They depend on what their friends or acquaintances say rather than strong factual research and knowledge on the investment. Avoid this herd mentality. Just because there are large groups of people rushing towards the investment like a herd of wildebeest doesn't make it a good investment, let alone a great one. Everyone could be rushing towards a big con or a bad investment waiting to crash. Don't skip the fundamentals, research the investment and know how it works. Avoid rushing in due to a herd mentality, but work through a solid research plan that validates your reason for entering the investment.

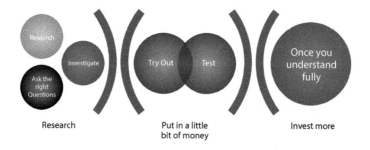

Research   Put in a little   Invest more
                  bit of money

4. Lack of Investment Testing

Let's say that you have done all the basics, your research plan is done, you know how the investment generates a return, the investment is legal, and you have done all the homework, and ticked all the boxes. The last thing you need to do is test. Spend time watching and testing the investment without using any real money.

Before I invested in the share market, I actually mirrored the market. I followed investments I hypothetically "bought" shares without using any actual cash. Too many people rush into an investment after reading a book or listening to an 'expert'. Theoretically, if I lose $100, 000 in an investment, I may be able to make it back through another investment. Therefore, my risk tolerance level could be higher than yours. If you risk losing the same amount of money, could you afford to lose that money and make it back?

Experts speak from their own high level of risk tolerance. You may not be able to take the same type of risks they are able to. It is best that you test your new found acumen by seeing how well you do in hypothetical situations rather than losing actual cash.

Give yourself a time period and see how well you do. When you stop losing and start making decisions that make sense and produces hypothetical wins, then you can enter into the market with some real money.

This is something we can do with our children as well. Perhaps while they are saving up cash for investment, you can mirror the markets together. Make theoretical decisions and see if you make or lose money.

Working the Economic Cycles

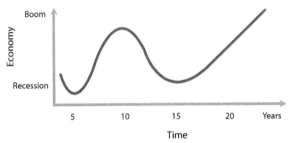

Economic Cycles go up and down sometimes once every five to seven years, some periods may take longer such as ten years. If you look at the graph above, you will realize that there is a time for you to go into an investment and buy it and also a time for you to get out of an investment and sell.

For example, if I buy a property during a recession period and sell it during a boom time I will make money. But here's the trick; we should teach our children not to buy another property straight away, but to hold on to the cash and wait for the next recession to buy again. From the money they have made and saved since the previous cycle, they could actually buy four properties, provided they are low end and in good locations, during the next recession as people will need the cash. Then wait again for the next boom time before selling those new properties. They could be multiplying their money many times over just by playing the economic cycles.

Through buying during recession periods and selling during boom periods we are able to multiply our money more compared to if we merely bought property at whatever time and waited for prices to go up.

I personally know someone who raised a fortune of $ 3, 000, 000 in fully paid up properties over 20 years because he used the economic cycles. The best part is that he did it only earning a salary of $ 2, 000 a month.

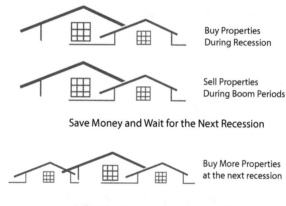

Buy Properties
During Recession

Sell Properties
During Boom Periods

Save Money and Wait for the Next Recession

Buy More Properties
at the next recession

Sell at the Next Boom and Repeat Process!

Risk Profiling Questionnaire

Answer, or ask your children to answer, the following questions and see which category you fit into. The interpretation for the answers is given below the questions. Bear in mind that children and youth are generally more adventurous and more willing to take risks as they are still young. That is fine, because if they lose some money, they may become a little more cautious in the future. Allow them freedom to express themselves and to face some consequences.

Risk Profiling Questionnaire

Questions

1. If you had $1 Million what would you prefer?

    a. An investment with a fixed return of 5% per year.

    b. An investment with a potential of 20% per year, but with a slight chance it might fail and you lose 50% of your capital.

    c. An investment that could potentially bring you a return of 70% within two years, but you might lose it all.

2. If you had a choice, which would be your first preference?

    a. Buying a house that can double in value in ten years (probability 100%)

    b. Buy a piece of land that could double its value in two years (probability 80%)

    c. Buy shares that could increase in value by 200% in one year or less (probability 50%)

3. You have time to...

    a. Look at your investments and track them once a month.

    b. Check your investments once in a while when needed and advised by your financial planner.

    c. You have access to your investments any time and you can track the markets real time.

4. Your tolerance makes you consider the following:

    a. I do not like to lose money and my capital.

    b. I focus on not losing as much as gaining money.

    c. I am only focused on gaining money.

5. Imagine that the stock market just crashed and you lost 25% of your capital, what is your next step?

    a. Cut your losses, sell your shares at a loss and cash out.

      b. Sell some of your shares, and keep some longer.

      c. Buy more shares.

6. Which of the following best describes your view of your retirement plan account?

      a. I am concerned about my investments losing value.

      b. I am equally concerned about my investments losing value and gaining value.

      c. I am most concerned about my investments gaining value.

7. I would say my knowledge on investments and my portfolio are:

      a. Non-existent

      b. Limited but passable

      c. Extensive

Interpretation of Your Answers and Your Risk Profile

Risk	Answers
Averse to Risk	All a)
Moderately Conservative	Half a) Half b)
Moderate	50% a) 25% b) 25% c)
Moderately Aggressive	25% c) and 75% b)
Aggressive	All c)

This is not a contest or a test for you to score on. There are no right answers to this; there are only true answers. You can still multiply your wealth greatly and achieve your financial goals regardless of your risk profile if you work according to your risk profile and make informed decisions.

It does not mean that high-risk takers will gain more or lose more. The key is making informed decisions based on a risk profile that suits your financial situation and the amount of finance you have.

This is vitally important.

Generally I would not recommend putting all your money in risky investments, nor putting all your money in totally safe investments. You are to find a balance that works for you. For example, putting 80% of your money in safe investments and 20% in risky ones might still lose you some money, but perhaps only with the 20% portion. The 80% might give you steady returns every year, but maybe only 6%. That is fine, however, choose the ratios according to what suits you. Always remember that you need to have more of your capital in safer steady investments that do not lose much value (like property in a great location for example).

Before we continue, let me first define what a risky investment is in terms of proper, informed financial multiplication principles.

A risky investment is one that is still financially sound that meets the criteria of a proper investment, legally as well as other criterion. It has a higher variation of possibilities of increase or decrease in terms of value, and a slightly higher volatile nature in terms of returns. Potential returns could also be delayed more than your expected time frame.

Factors that Inform Your Risk Profile

Generally your investments will all have a risk component. How much risk you should take depends on a few factors.

1. Age

Your age plays a role in your risk profile. You can generally take a bit more risk when you are younger and have time to recover if it fails.

2 Extra Funds Available

You still have some additional funds available after investing a considerable amount of capital in investments with a relatively steady return and medium to low risk profiles. If you want to take some risk with a small portion of your investments you are in a position to do so. If you put everything in low return investments, you will be safer than most, but your money also needs to multiply at a higher rate than inflation, which some people say is around 5% or more per annum.

3. Timeframe of Investment

The time you need to multiply an investment is an important factor that influences your risk profile.

It could be that you came into some money at fifty plus years of age and you have a limited time to multiply your money before you retire. If you find yourself in these sort of situations where you don't urgently need the money immediately, then it is important to take a few calculated risks (legal sound investments). Take time to put your money where it will multiply, and where you have some risks involved, but where the returns are there in time. The risk must be calculated, meaning you have done your homework and research well. You must also be able to recover from such situations financially if it does not turn out for the best.

Dangerous Investment Positions to Avoid

Even the best investments carry a measure of risk and there is always the chance that you might lose money. However, there are some situations that you must absolutely avoid to ensure that you are not in a position where you will lose money. By taking these precautions, you can put yourself in a safer position. These are some situations you must teach your children to undoubtedly avoid when it comes to investing or investments in order to mitigate your risk.

(I have used some well-known phrases as headings to help you remember these)

1. All the Eggs in One Basket

You have all your investments tied up in one major investment and no diversification.

For example, if you have all your money tied up in, let's say, one major property investment, you will be in a high-risk position. What happens if your investment does not pan out? Your entire investment portfolio for your future and everything else then fails due to being tied up in this one investment.

There are many who advocate that diversification is a safe policy when it comes to investments. If one of your eggs in one basket fails, you then still have others to use as back up.

2. Bad Timing

You have gone into an investment at the wrong time when it is peaking rather than when it is coming down.

Timing is everything when it comes to investments. We will be covering this more in detail when we talk about economic cycles. Just because you or your children have suddenly read or been educated on investment does not mean that now is the right time to enter the markets. Be patient, and don't rush. Figure out the best time to go in when prices have dropped a little and buy when it is lower.

3. Flying Blind

You have no understanding of the signs of recession and boom economic periods and are investing blind.

Most people have very little understanding of the economic periods of recession and growth, and do not know how to read the signs or read government reports that indicate when we are heading for a recession. These people are in a dangerous place because they can get caught with the wrong product at the wrong time.

4. Single Point of Failure

You have no liquidity or buffer for emergencies and every-thing is tied up in investments you cannot liquidate quickly.

Emergencies do happen and you have to expect them. When they do happen and you require cash, you have to have at least some at your disposal. You need to have an emergency cash fund available and a buffer to sustain you through the duration of the emergency.

One family I learnt this from had $ 2 Million they put in Fixed Deposits (F.D.) in small amounts of $ 60, 000 to $ 100, 000 on yearly or 24 month Fixed Deposits amounting to $ 2 Million in total. Every month they would have $60 000 to $100 000 available to use in case of an emergency and if they didn't need it, they would reinvest it for another year in F.D. If they ever needed cash it was always available.

In terms of a buffer, it is critical to have at least six months of your expenses ready in case you lose your source of income.

5. Blind Leading the Blind

You have gone into an investment because somebody ad-vised you or a group of friends have done so, but not because you have done your own research.

You need to be clear on why you are picking a specific in-vestment! Even if somebody gives you a tip, you still have to ensure that you are making an informed decision, not follow-ing someone else's tip. If you have done so, quickly do your research. Find out all you can about the investment. If you find out you have made the right decision and came in at the right time, then stick with it, if not find a way to liquidate this and get out of it fast.

It is critical that both you and your children are able to iden-tify dangerous investment situations so that you can avoid them in your journey towards creating wealth. If you already find yourself in a dangerous financial position, find a way to get out of it fast. Sell or divest the investment to recoup your capital as quickly as you can.

Scams – What to Look Out for and How to Avoid Them

We don't want our children to be cheated, therefore we must always be on the lookout for scams. Teach them how to identify a potential scam and how to avoid losing money through those scams.

Recently in the US there have been some high profile cases of people running what they claimed to be investment funds or hedge funds, which actually turned out to be scams. Billions of dollars were lost through the scams of these fraudsters. I won't mention names here as some of them are still under investigation, but you can Google it for yourself.

Human greed works on both sides of the divide. Conmen are greedy and want to make money fast, even if it means compromising principles.

In most cases the people who invest in a con also give in to greed and take risks they should not. Sometimes they are genuine victims who just lack education. While people who are cheated should not be blamed for their losses, they could certainly have avoided it with proper education. You must always know and understand what you are investing in and how the investment works.

Be suspicious of so-called investments that have the following:

1. Promise of Disproportional Returns

Be very careful of "investments" that promise astronomical or disproportional returns in unrealistic timeframes.

People say if an investment promises more than 3.5% per month, it could be a scam. You need to clearly understand how the investment is generating a return.

2. Investments that Keep Recruiting

Investments that aggressively keep trying to recruit more people, could also be a ponzi scheme. A ponzi scheme is a con that keeps taking in new money from new investors to pay out to old investors claiming high returns. It actually builds up until the total investment from the recruitment of people reaches a climax, then the conmen disappear with all the money.

3. Vague or Non-Transparent Investments

When the promoters of the investment are vague, shifty and not transparent with you.

Whenever you ask questions, especially questions such as how the investment makes money, you should get a straight answer. So, when people are shifty or not being transparent with you, something could be wrong. It could well be a con.

4. Overly Dependant on Reputation and Endorsements

When people rely on the reputation of others and on brand names rather than the investment itself giving a return.

Good people sometimes get their names dragged into a bad investment. They could be celebrities or members of society in good standing, but because conmen have found a way to associate with them or use these big names, others can be pulled into the con. It is not that these endorsers are bad people, it is simply that they can also be conned. Any investment you are considering must have a good model of generating money by itself and must hold actual financial value.

5. Investments by Unknown Entities

When it is an organization or institution running investments you haven't heard about, you should see that as a cause for concern.

If it is new, and promising a lot in returns, check it out thoroughly first before jumping in. In most countries, investment organizations and financial institutions that promote and run investments are very well regulated. Chances are that a new player that is not registered with the regulatory bodies could be a con. Be careful and research the organizations you are investing in. Look into their board of directors, registration documents, paid up capital or cash reserves. Many of these records are in the public domain and you can find them out for yourself.

EXERCISE: Investment 101
Basic Rules for Multiplying Wealth

For Ages 5-9

Explain an investment area you are comfortable with in simple steps without great detail. Such as shares or investment funds that are sold in units. It could also be a property or a land investment. The key is to explain it in simple terms and show them money when explaining multiplication.

For example:

This is a share we are going to buy with this $10. When we buy this share it means we own a small part of this business. The share can go up in value (show them another few $10 notes).

We buy this in the share market. It is like the market where we buy our vegetables and meat, but this market only sells ownership in companies.

We might lose money (now take away some $10 notes) or we might win more money (add more $10 notes).

You need to be a big business to sell your shares in the share market. Do you want to invest a portion of your money from your savings together with me after we learn and do some research to choose the right company so we can grow our money?

If we just keep our money here and don't invest it (explain investment as buying something we can sell for more money), we don't grow our money (Point to a tree, and talk about the tree analogy and teach them that multiplication means, your money gets more and more like the tree grows).

For Ages 10-17

1. Develop a research plan with your child to study a particular investment for a period of six to twelve months. Do research according to the categories listed below:

2. When you are ready and have followed your research plan and exercised due diligence, track the investment without using real money. Play it like a game with your children. How much did you make after one year?

3. You and your child are now ready to take the step to invest provided you and your child are comfortable with the particular investment and with the risk it carries (It is important to find something that you know well so that you can invest in it together with your child and also be able to guide your child).

4. Put your money and a small portion of your child's into an investment that you can do together. It could be a share, small business, or even a hedge fund or unit trust investment. We want something small to start off with, however, if you feel you and your children are ready and have the capital, it could even be a property or land where you come up with the majority of the money and your children come up with the rest.

5. While working on this as one project with your children, you can continue to work on other projects with them as well. Let them be excited about multiplying their money together with you. You just need to be comfortable with the risk you are taking and the returns you are expecting. Don't jump into investments which are too risky for you or your children. Let them enjoy the experience and keep doing this with them for as long as you can.

6. When you lose money, learn the lesson together and look for the next investment opportunity that can pan out for you and multiply your money. Keep your children excited and keep learning and researching together about the field you are in.

The investment	Expected ROI	What are the risk factors?
How does this investment generate a return?	How much are you investing?	How much do you want to make from this investment?
What is your exit strategy?	When is the right time to go into the investment?	How much are you willing to lose and how long are you willing to wait if the investment does not pan out?

Chapter 8

Debt Management
Making Use of Credit Systems to Win

In every society today in almost every nation we see an increase in household debt. There are two reasons for this: The first being easier access to loans, and the second being the pressure on people to live an affluent lifestyle that compels them to buy things they cannot afford on credit. Today you can lease or rent cars, vacation homes, and even furniture.

There are many people who swear that debt is a bad thing, however, another person I talked to, an economist, has a theory that being in debt is not bad because you reserve your own cash to use during a recession.

I believe that there is *Good Debt* and *Bad Debt* and that it is important to understand the difference between the two.

Let's look at both and what the differences are between them.

Good Debt

1. Borrowing to Achieve Wealth Goals

Good debt is borrowing for the short-term in order to achieve a financial goal.

Why is the phrase 'short-term' important? Because most loans or debts with a longer repayment tenure causes you to pay more, in interest, for what you are purchasing. If you are taking any loan it is important to pay it off as fast as possible so that you don't pay too much in interest.

For example, some housing loans with a very long repayment tenure look good to you because your monthly installments appear small. What looks affordable in the short-term actually adds up in the long-term. The longer the term, the higher the interest rates. This is something you need to teach your children. Some loans actually charge interest that amounts to three times the value of the property you are buying if you use it for the entire tenure of, let's say, 30-40 years.

Some banks in certain countries are even coming up with loans that allow a parent to buy a property and then live in it and pass on the debt to their children when they are older. To be borrowing off the names and future of your children and saddling them with debt even before they earn their own income. That is a really bad thing to do.

2. Borrow for Appreciating Assets

Make use of loans for acquiring appreciating, not depreciating assets.

Using a loan for an appreciating asset such as a property is fine, but buying a car with a loan is a bad thing. Most people however use loans to buy cars. The minute that you buy a car and drive out of the showroom, the value of your vehicle could go down as much as 30%. This loss of value makes cars a depreciating asset.

In Malaysia, the Government encourages buying cars as part of its automotive development policy. You are allowed, as a business person with profits in your company, to buy cars and deduct the value of that car (up to $100, 000) from your taxable income over four years. Terms and Conditions apply, but the Government has allowed this in order to increase the sales of nationally manufactured cars. In such a situation, if you actually need a car and if your company have a profit and are within the boundaries of economic sense, then you can buy it and deduct it within the legal framework of tax deductions and follow the scale.

The tax scale for luxury cars in Malaysia is also very high, and in some cases can be up to 300% more than the price of the car. Yet, more and more people are getting into debt, borrowing money to buy these high priced cars, defaulting on the loans, having the cars repossessed and becoming bankrupt for the balance they owe. Statistics are showing the majority of those who default are young adults.

Your children should learn to borrow for appreciating assets. Imagine if they bought a house in a good location, even during a bad economic climate. That house has value and could be in demand (irrespective of the downturn), thereby reducing the risk of being unable to cover their loan payments when in a pinch. They could sell the property they own if they need cash, or rent it out for regular monthly income.

Teach your children about different housing loans available and when the best times are for using the different options. There are times that they will need loans either with fixed interest rates, sliding scale, or rates according to a base lending rate fixed by government authorities and market sentiment. Each has different advantages and disadvantages, during economic crisis and boom times.

3. Borrow to Afford Needful Long-Term Purchases

Use the convenience of loans to purchase things that are affordable for you in the long term.

There are always different things that you are going to need to survive. The three basic things most people need to survive are:

- Food
- Shelter
- Transport

You should not be borrowing money for food, and we do not advise borrowing money for transport or cars unless there are tax advantages or other loopholes you can legally take advantage of. However, you are always going to need a house. Sometimes you may not be able to save up the amount of money you will need to purchase a house in a short time frame.

You cannot wait until you have saved up $ 300 000 to buy a house cash. Therefore, a loan offers the convenience of buying the right property in a price range suitable for you so that you have a place to live. As you repay the loan you begin to own the house (although you don't actually own it until every cent is paid off).

4. Good Debt to Income Ratios

Stay within good debt to income ratios. A good yardstick of your total debt repayment should never exceed than 40% of your income. This is so you can always have positive cash flow for your wealth multiplier account. With too much debt you end up having all your hard earned cash servicing interest for loans.

Buying everything cash is also going to inconvenience you sometimes. As with the example I gave you above; you would probably need to save for a lifetime before you would be able to buy a house if you have to do it cash. Teach your children how to use the convenience of a loan, but also how to be accountable to pay it back.

If 40% or less of your total income is spent servicing your

loans and debt, it means you have 60% to live off. Your amount of capital that you can create for investment from your monthly income is going to be very minimal. This causes you to be in debt longer and keeps you in a cycle where very little investments are made. Without adequate investment capital, you can generate only very minimal amounts of wealth for yourself.

5. Borrowing Only for Guaranteed Return Investments

Borrowing money to invest in fixed return or guaranteed return assets and investments.

If you borrow money at a fixed interest rate, and have fixed income coming in every month as a guarantee, and the money being paid to you by the investment is higher than the interest on the loan, then it is worth taking a loan.

In some countries there are feed in tariff systems for solar power. Basically, the Government endeavors to raise more green or renewable energy for consumer consumption. They then begin to allow private individuals to put solar power panels on their roofs to generate and supply electricity back to the central power grid for a fee. In some countries like Malaysia it can be at a fixed rate for twenty-one years.

Study the quality of the products and the systems well to know your rights before you do it. Reread section on the foundations for investment research that is covered in the chapters on investment before you invest.

There are many other deals like this that you can take advantage of. For example, I once invested in a low priced apartment next to a rail transit station. Because it is a major transport hub, it was a highly tenantable apartment where a vacancy could easily be filled within a day, or sometimes within an hour. The rental income was constant even in a recession. Borrowing money for these types of investments are more profitable than others with returns that can vary.

Borrow fro Appreciative Assets

Things that multiply with guaranteed returns higher than the interest for borrowing

Pay off as fast as possible

Reduce your loan tenure and pay off loans faster if possible

Use the system

Don't let the system use you by keeping you in high debt for longer and longer periods, borrow and finish paying off loans fast to beat the system

Bad Debt

1. Borrowing for Depreciating Assets

Using debt for buying depreciating assets is a bad debt.

When you take out loans for depreciating assets (assets that lose value over time and do not appreciate in value or give you any extra income) and you have to pay not only the principal purchase amount but interest as well, then you lose. Examples of such items are car loans, or credit card installments for the latest designer handbag etc. With this you end up using more productive money to service interest on loans for unproductive items rather than for investments that can generate more money.

Money you work for should be used to work for you! You should be using the majority of it for appreciating assets. You need to teach your children that some of the depreciating assets that people buy are very much linked to their emotional state. They buy to make themselves feel good, or they buy because they cannot wait and practice delayed gratification. When you or your children learn to deal with these issues, you will be less likely to waste money on depreciating items.

2. Cash Advances and Borrowing Without Collateral

Taking debt without collateral, such as cash advances with high interest rates are bad debts.

Cash advances are one of the worst things to do with your credit cards. A credit card is meant to be used and paid off in full at the end of each month. When you carry your balances forward or take cash advances on your credit card, you then get into a position where you have debt without any collateral.

Banks know that if you don't have collateral, they are taking a bigger risk with you. The higher the bank's risk, the more interest they will charge you. Be very careful and don't be too glad when you are offered a high interest cash advance or loan without capital. It is dangerous, and some loans charge up to 75% interest on the principle amount taken over the tenure of the loan.

If you need cash; work for it! Save up for emergencies, follow the principles in this book, and teach your children to follow them as well, so that they the Money Quotient to avoid the traps that get people tied up in so many bad debts.

3. Using Borrowings for Wrong Purposes

Using funds taken as loans for something other than the purpose for which it was borrowed is very bad debt.

People sometimes take loans meant for a particular purpose and then use it for a different (wrong) purposes. For example, I know people who have taken small micro business loans, meant to be used to kick-start their business venture or their business expansion taking it to the next level to generate more income. Instead, they used it for other purposes that do not generate income. They used it as a down payment for a car, or used it to buy fancy laptop computers or smart phones, fashionable products, and other types of purchases driven by emotional desires. It is used for every type of purpose except the one for which it was intended.

I am talking about people who would probably struggle to pay off the micro loan in the first place. So, instead of using the loan to push up their incomes to a higher level, they saddled themselves with more debt to pay off before even being able to save money for some capital to use in investments. The purpose for a loan is very important and certain loans have high interest rates, which are only possible to service if you are generating enough cash returns from the loan, such as business loans without collateral.

4. Hire Purchase

I am strongly against people buying furniture or phones, computers and other items on hire purchase. This is because of the fact being that the hire purchase companies have to charge high interest rates. They are taking huge risks giving people they don't know products which their company has to pay for. Thus to mitigate their risk, as they will not be able to collect from all defaulters, they charge you more to cover the loss from others.

If you make use of hire purchase, you end up paying twice or three times the value of the product in some instances. Buying a computer on hire purchase is a bad idea because the interest can be double or triple the cash value of the item. You end up paying so much more for an item that is worth less. I have a simple fail proof rule you can teach to your children. If you cannot afford it, don't buy it! Getting into debt for a lounge chair is not going to be relaxing when you default!

5. Margin Financing to Buy Shares

Using short-term loans such as margin financing to buy shares and other investments is bad debt.

Some people say that it is good to use other people's money (OPM) to make more money. Well, if you have saved up and built capital, why not use your own? If you use other people's money you still have to pay them back with interest. If you use your own money and accumulated capital because of your adjusted lifestyle, the money you make in returns goes straight to you.

The more you save, the more capital you have, the more you invest, the more of your money you have working for you.

Margin financing was a great buzz-word in Malaysia in the past. It allowed people to buy shares and take risks without having to come up with their own money. In certain good economic climates in Malaysia, everyone was doing it and they were doing it with billions of dollars in loans. However, when the financial crunch came, many high profile individuals got caught. Recessions always come, and you need to avoid over-extending yourself. One of the main reasons people borrow more and more money and take greater and greater risk is simply put, greed.

Best Practices When Taking Loans

Teach your children these best practices when taking out loans and make sure you also model them so that you and your children can beat the system.

1. Pay Debt Off As Fast As Possible

When you have a loan, pay it off faster to reduce your interest. This enables you to sell or dispose of your property or investment whenever you need to. Paying off a loan faster also makes you more resilient to survive a credit crunch better, as you do not have many overheads during a recession period and can live on less.

2. Pay Bigger Deposits

Pay a bigger deposit when taking a loan so that your installments are smaller and finish faster.

This is important because the smaller the deposit you pay on a loan, such as a property loan, the higher the monthly burden you will have to bear each month, and the higher the amount of interest you have to pay. Increasing your deposit on a loan reduces interest and your monthly financial burden significantly.

3.   Do NOT Over-Extend Your Credit

When you take a loan, it is NOT free money! You have to pay it back! I know people who have taken big loans to buy luxurious cars, and bungalows only to get into trouble because their income levels cannot service such a loan. Don't over-extend. Borrow only what you can afford to pay back.

4.   Do NOT Buy Too Many Properties on Debt

Stacking too many properties and doing so on debt can leave you vulnerable in the event that cash flow constrained.

I know someone who bought three properties on high loans. First of all, you do not own any property unless you have paid it off in full and had the charge on your property from the bank removed.

Imagine this scenario; if all your loans are recalled, you lose everything at once. Imagine another scenario; if you lose your job and are unable to pay the monthly installments, you can also lose all your properties at once.

Therefore, pay off some properties or loans first before getting yourself into more debt with other properties.

5.   NEVER Take Credit Card Cash Advances

This is one of the most dangerous things you can ever do financially. Cash advances from credit cards have some of the highest interest rates around.

If you need cash, then find some other source. Better yet, do not borrow, but live a lifestyle below your means and save so that you can have access to cash when you need it. Also remember that you need to have at least six months of your expenses saved up in cash you have ready access to in case you get into any emergency situation. This is called a buffer.

6. Look Around for the Best Deal

Shop around and get the best deal, rates and benefits, and ask the banks to explain all terms conditions and different types of loans to you.

It is your right as a consumer to get the best deal for yourself. If one bank offers you a low interest rate use it to negotiate for an even lower rate with another bank. Find the best deal and best fit to suit your needs.

As a consumer it is also your right to have the bank explain everything you need to know thoroughly, especially the terms and conditions you do not understand. If they don't, then make a complaint and take it to the authorities and don't sign with them but look elsewhere.

7. Secure Loan Pre-Approval

Get pre-approved for loans even before making large purchases that require financing.

When you are going to make a property or a car purchase on loan, you can also negotiate with your bank to see what loan amount you can get and at what interest rate before the purchase decision. You do not want to be in a situation where you have paid the down payment but then unable to get the loan for the rest. Otherwise you will have to run everywhere trying to borrow money to pay the balance, or even risk losing your down payment due to time limits stipulated in your initial down payment contract giving you only a short period to obtain financing.

8. Keep a Clean Credit History

Keep your credit history clean and in the clear by paying off all loans on time.

Pay your installments on time. Never default, because if you have a bad credit history, you will not get the best rates and deals for loans. In fact, banks might not want to lend you anything at all because you are deemed an irresponsible credit risk.

Pay one month in advance, so that if there is an emergency you have a one-month buffer. Have a good credit testimony that you can use to get a loan for other appreciating items when you need to.

9. Use the Economic Cycles

Switch to a fixed interest loan during a recession and to a flexi interest loan with a sliding scale interest rate during boom times to save you money on interest (provided you don't lose money or have to pay a penalty when you switch). Working on the type of loans you have at different periods will bring the cost of servicing your loan down.

10. Be Proactive When Caught in Difficult Times

When in extreme difficulty and you are unable to pay off loans, chase after the banks instead of the banks chasing after you.

This will show you are sincere about clearing your debt. Talk to the banks about what you can afford to pay. Cancel your credit cards if you are in high credit card debt and convert them into a loan with lower interest rates and pay this off as fast as you can.

11. Get Government Approved Help When in Distress

Make use of approved government credit agencies when in financial distress.

Increasingly, governments are setting up agencies to help those with high debt and also to negotiate on their behalf to repay those debts. In Malaysia there is a government agency called AKPK that has an understanding with all banks. When you approach them with credit card debt, you are immediately put on a debt repayment plan that is pre-negotiated with the banks. You are given a debt settlement amount to pay off with a reduced interest scale, all your credit cards are cancelled and you are given a fixed time and payment amount to pay towards this settlement.

AKPK in Malaysia and similar debt management agencies in other countries are set up to assist those who have fallen into bad debt. They have pre-negotiated settlement plans and other special authorities to negotiate with banks on your behalf in certain circumstances where interest reductions are needed.

12. Avoid Living On Debt and Credit

Live on cash as much as possible not on loans and credit.

I know someone who used to earn $10, 000 a month and spent $11, 000 a month, most of it on his credit card. He is bankrupt today. The temptation to think that credit cards are extra cash for you to spend is causing so many young people across the nations to get into debt. "Live for the moment, worry about the consequences later", is a spirit that is invading the mindset of our young people and causing them to think and live short-term enjoyment, instead of living with the hope of a better financial future through practicing the right financial principles.

Credit Cards. Do You Need Them?

One of the fastest ways our children can get into debt is through credit cards. There are more people today getting bankrupt through credit card misusage than ever before. In some countries, people are having five to seven cards and are in between $55 000 to $60 000 in debt on average. With the advent of the internet and air travel being more accessible, credit cards offer a definite convenience. However, if you have a lifestyle and financial habits that violate sound financial principles and you have a credit card, you are more likely in serious danger of getting into bad credit card debt.

Here are some tips when using credit cards:

- It is a good tool only if it is used well.
- If you have bad money management habits DO NOT own a credit card.
- Never carry a balance forward! Pay off your debt in full every month.
- NEVER take a cash advance from your credit card!
- Credit cards are loans! They are NOT free money! You have to pay everything back with interest.
- Never have or own more than two credit cards.
- Take each card from a different bank. If there is a problem and the systems is down at one bank you have access to another.

Key Thoughts On Credit Cards

EXERCISE: Debt Management
Making Use of Credit Systems to Win

For All Ages

Tell your child that you are going to give them a loan to buy whatever they want up to a certain ceiling amount. It must be for something they don't need, but want. We want to work with wrong desires and get them into a little bit of trouble. Be prepared for emotional outbursts and your child showing disappointment when they have to face realities of the financial pressure you are going to simulate for them later. Stay focused and follow through, and remember this is going to be a lesson that will prepare them for real life. You are empowering your child by creating this experience for them.

To define this ceiling amount you need to take the following factors into consideration:

1. You know what your child likes and this figure must be able to excite them and give them enough money to buy a reasonable item they ask for

2. You basically want them to borrow from you, if the item you suggest is not exciting they will not buy it

3. It could be a toy for a younger child or an iPod or a simple smart phone for an older child.

4. It must take into account your own financial state and what you can afford to give as a loan

5. You also have to take your child's age into account. It is easier to excite the younger ones than the older.

6. Most importantly your children must be able to pay you back, via their pocket money, however, not too easily. This exercise seeks to put pressure on them

Choose the Item

1. Choose an item within a reasonable price range using the guidelines given above.

2. Remember it has to be an item your child is excited about

3. Offer a loan to your child that they have to repay so that they can get the item they want now

4. Tell them there is an existing interest rate of 30% and that this could go up or down with the financial market you have to simulate

5. Gloss over the last point above quickly and not in detail so you can get them hooked on buying with credit

6. Write out a simple 1 page loan agreement and work out the repayment terms for every week etc. based on what pocket money your child earns

7. Include in the terms and conditions this key term *"the lender reserves the right to allow for early settlement of the loan and to offer prevailing interest rates according to market conditions decided by the buyer. Rates may be lower or higher to simulate market conditions and are subject to the lenders interpretation of market demands."*

8. After they sign the loan agreement with the term that allows for you to increase interest rates, lend them the money, go with them and pay for the item

9. Walk to the counter with the child and give them the cash to pay for it

10. Your child must physically hold the money

11. Collect back money at the agreed sum by deducting it from their pocket money

12. Your child must feel a slight pinch, so its good to deduct 30-50% of their pocket money to repay the loan, therefore the loan amount and tenure should be worked out based on the 30-50% repayment you want to achieve

Simulate a Financial Crash

Reduce their pocket money by half. Explain that there is a financial crises in the economy (in real life people can lose jobs and be forced to take pay cuts).

The idea is to make sure they cannot repay you back with the new pressures you are adding on. You can also increase interest rates to 70% or more and demand the same repayment tenure, so they have to pay you back more, if you can explain interest rates in a way they can understand (for younger children, take one $ 10 note and one $ 5 and tell them if they borrow $ 10 this they have to pay back interest which is $ 10 + $5 = $15).

During this period make sure their health is not compromised. Ensure that they take food from home for school breaks if they do not have money to pay for lunches or breaks. You can even communicate your plan and what you are doing to your child's teachers so they can keep an eye on your child and work with you.

You can also take money from next weeks pocket money if they are short so tell them they get nothing the following week

They have to eat at school, so you tell them that you have to repossess the purchased item temporarily. If they cannot pay you back (which is the ideal situation) Put it somewhere where they can see it, but do not let them play with it or use it. However, still do not give them their pocket money for a week or give only the reduced sum that gets less and less.

The idea is to change the rules and pile on pressure to repay more that what was initially agreed. If they complain, bring out the agreement. Keep raising the interest rates little by little until they cannot repay and have to completely forfeit the item to you.

After the pain, the explanation you give your child can be as follows:

Never borrow for depreciative items, tell them that people borrow money from credit cards, take personal loans to buy things they want and not things they need. If you borrow to buy a house in a good location, you can do so.

However, remember banks can change interest rates according to government policy and this can go up significantly and hurt you financially if you are over extended. In some countries, banks can even recall a loan without giving any reasons.

Explain the key principles in this chapter, such as borrowing for appreciating assets and never overextending by taking too much credit so that they don't get caught like they did ever again.

Explain to them most loan agreements for houses and cars are very one sided and in favor of the bank and the lender who needs to be protected because they are lending to everybody who is untested. Sometimes with some banks in certain countries, it is a little too much in the lenders' favor. Tell them the key to beat the system is for them to pay a high downpayment for the loan, and shop around and compare rates with other banks. This will enable them to get the best rates and reduce the interest of overall loan.

This exercise will stay with your child for life and they will remember it every time they want to borrow money from a lending institution. From time to time you can repeat it especially if your child was young at the time of the first exercise.

Chapter 9

Working the Economic Cycles

Money Management in a Recession

Recessions are not necessarily bad times because they are great times to multiply wealth provided that one is prepared and has sufficient cash to plunder the opportunities. Your children need to be familiar with the basic concept of each cycle in order to understand how to create opportunities and safety nets for themselves to both survive and thrive during each cycle.

As mentioned earlier, every nation will go through an up or down cycle with its own economy. The trend is usually 5-7 years of economic boom times where you can make money easily, and 5-7 years of recession thereafter where making money becomes extremely difficult. In a recession cash flow becomes a problem and people do not usually have ready cash on hand to capitalize on opportunities.

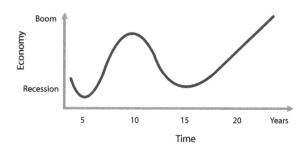

There is one exception to the rule however and that is if a government does not improve confidence through accurate economic policies during a recession, a downturn can turn into a depression, which we saw in the US in the 1930s and recently in Greece. This is a horrible state to be in where there are no investments in the country, the whole economic systems have collapsed, and even the currency might crash and lose almost all of its value. In Argentina some years ago, the value of currency was so low that ridiculous amounts had to be paid just to buy a washing machine because of the extreme devaluation of the currency.

Whether you are in a recession or, in a worst case scenario, a depression, the key is to make preparations in each cycle so that you can thrive or survive in the next cycle.

Let's say for example that we have 7 years of economic boom time, 7 years of recession and about 4-5 years of depression or collapse of the economic systems. The following are what you can do and how you can prepare for each cycle so that you can capitalize and take over opportunities, and survive and thrive during the crash.

You must find and make your own preparations to be ready for each cycle, and not just follow a trend or even what I am saying as the "end-all" of preparation. Research this topic and related investments thoroughly so that you make decisions based on your own economic state, risk potential, and financial knowledge. You must teach your children not to rush into decisions but take the time to adequately plan and prepare their strategies.

Thoughts to be Mindful of in Preparation for Each Cycle

Some preparations to consider include, but are not limited to the following:

1. What To Invest in and What To Avoid

We must be mindful of what to invest in and what not. Investments with long periods before any return can be seen must be avoided. For example, any investment with a ten-year return, during a seven-year expected boom period should be avoided. We need to use common sense and not be taken up by marketing materials of investments with returns not happening within timelines that we have set.

2. Business ROI Timeframe

Businesses must be started with specific time frames to capitalize. For example, if you have seven good years during a boom period with a recession following after, you must get a good return on investment for the business within those seven years, and the return must be enough to tide you over during the recession period and get you through it.

3. Long-Term and Big Investments

Things such as houses or cars may need to be deferred and capital utilized for investments with a shorter return during the boom period, or for investments that are safe and revenue spinning even during a recession.

4. Savings and Money Management

Lifestyles spending and other expenditures need to be cut down or readjusted to a reasonable level in preparation of a recession to come. This is because savings need to be increased. The more you spend, the less you save, and this is what gets you into trouble when a recession or depression hits.

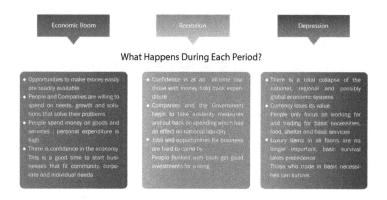

What Happens During Each Period?

Economic Boom	Recession	Depression
• Opportunities to make money easily are readily available • People and Companies are willing to spend on needs, growth and solutions that solve their problems • People spend money on goods and services ; personal expenditure is high • There is confidence in the economy This is a good time to start businesses that fit community, corporate and individual needs	• Confidence is at an all-time low; those with money hold back expenditure • Companies and the Government begin to take austerity measures and cut back on spending which has an effect on national liquidity • Jobs and opportunities for business are hard to come by People flushed with cash get good investments for a song	• There is a total collapse of the national, regional and possibly global economic systems • Currency loses its value People only focus on working for and trading for basic necessities, food, shelter and basic services • Luxury items in all forms are no longer important, basic survival takes precedence Those who trade in basic necessities can survive.

What You Can Do During Economic Boom Times

1. Save 20%

One of the most important things I learnt from my mentor, Dr. Jonathan David, is to save 20% of your income and put it aside for the recession when it comes, and believe me it will come.

2. Look for Opportunities With Quick ROI

Look for opportunities; investments and businesses to invest in or start with a quick return on investment.

The faster the return the better. For example, if there is a business that can give you a guaranteed return of 30% annually because the industry is in a growth phase, do your research to make sure it is not a scam, and invest in it if it is legitimate.

3. Do NOT Over-extend

Do not over-extend on your use of credit facilities. In good times credit is easy to come by. People have more money so they buy extravagant houses, big cars, and make investments by being super-positive and not realistic. We, and our children, must understand that good times do not last forever and we must live to prepare for the recession that will come.

4. Pay Off Unnecessary Debt Fast

Pay off all unnecessary debt as fast as you possibly can. Owning a house is a good thing, a loan from a bank helps you work towards that ownership. However, getting into too much unnecessary debt, buying too many properties on credit, buying expensive cars on credit, and having huge credit card bills, all lead to significant added pressure on your finances during a recession. The key is to live a moderate lifestyle, as I have mentioned in the previous chapters, and to live as if there is no significant increase even in the boom times so that you can save money during that time and wait for opportunities during the recession follows.

5. Be Selective With Available Opportunities

Don't jump into every opportunity that presents itself.

Learn to discern what good opportunities are and what are not. Go through the rules of investment that I have outlined in Chapter Seven and use them to analyze the opportunity to see if it is really safe. There is a danger of putting your resources, time and energy into the wrong opportunities during a boom period because everything looks good from the outside. Learn to look at opportunities via a seven-year cycle and plan for the recession to come. It is also critical that you do not overextend your resources, finances and time by committing to and taking up too many opportunities.

6. Balance Good Investments With Cash Reserves

While making good investments to multiply money, also look at just building up a cash reserve.

During a recession cash is king. If you miss the signs and are suddenly plunged into a recession, money that is tied up in shares, houses, unit trusts, and financial instruments can suddenly lose value overnight. It is also difficult to liquidate these investments during a recession. Having a portion of your savings in plain simple cash is important as a preparation for a recession.

7. Multiply Results Through Networking and Collaboration

Learn how to network and work with people to duplicate results without stretching your resources.

During the time of economic boom there will be plenty of opportunities and you will not have the time, resources, or ability to take up every one of them. However, if you can get good friends or a network of safe people to work with you can duplicate and add strength to each other. As a group, people can take advantage of more opportunities than individuals can. You have heard the old adage, that there is strength in numbers, well it's true. If there are five of you who can work together to start three businesses with the finance person around you managing the finances of all three businesses, and three of you sell and one administrates the delivery of products and services, then each of you can join together to start three strong businesses instead of just one weak one. Another thing you can do, if you have contacts and a network of influence and financial resources, is to kick start people of character and a good work ethic into starting and working businesses for you. This way you can use money to multiply money and your resource of contacts to supernaturally increase what you have, rather than sitting on a pile of cash that is doing nothing for you during a boom period.

8. Liquidate at the Right Time

Learn to liquidate at the right time by reading the signs.

When governments start cutting expenditure, predict negative growth rates, bring interest rates down dramatically, and when government bonds suddenly raise their returns, these could be signs that a recession is coming. We must learn to read through mirrors and smoke to understand what is actually happening with the economy and make our preparations. The last thing you want happening to you is to be saddled with huge investments in the share market and other investments when everything is losing its value and on a downturn. If you convert your investments to cash before the market crashes you will have cash and resources to plunder before a recession.

What You Can Do During a Recession

As I mentioned earlier, recessions are not necessarily bad periods if you have been managing your money strategically using the economic cycles as a base for planning. Many wealthy people understand how to use the cycles and grow their wealth by three or four times during a recession. Below are some ideas as to what you can do during a recession, these are by no means complete, you can add to it or adapt it to suit your requirements. If your children understand this and know how to set themselves up and take advantage of a recession when they are older, they are more likely to thrive compared to their uneducated peers.

Here are some strategies how you can set yourself up well in a recession:

1. Have Cash to Buy up Bargains

Use the cash that you have to buy into and take up opportunities that are bargains in terms of market value and that have good returns even during a recession. Low cost apartments with tenants in good locations might prove to be worthwhile after you do your research. So may blocks of land also be that are in great up-and-coming locations.

Luxury property, however, might not give you adequate returns or be able to pay for itself because it could be difficult to rent out. If you buy them during a recession, it must be an absolute bargain that you can capitalize on. Don't be too quick to buy luxury items that you cannot dispose of quickly for cash. You do not want to be saddled with bad buying decisions and a lack of liquidity to take advantage of other opportunities. However, recognize that there will be bargains and opportunities for you, so keep your eyes and ears open.

2. Prioritize Cash Flow and Safe ROI

Everything must be looked at from a perspective of generating cash flow and safe returns on investments. This is not the time to take uncalculated risks. If you put all your money into investments that are not generating returns, soon all your cash will be used to keep these investments going and nothing will be coming back to you. Worse still, some of these investments might even lose more value, because they have not bottomed out yet, this will create more pressure in your financial state. There are good investments you can take advantage of. For example, if there is a diner or a low cost eatery that is extremely popular, or a business that helps companies reduce costs dramatically, yet they are looking for some additional cash flow, these could be good business investments. Other good investments include low cost apartments with good transport infrastructure nearby such as trains. Rental yields in such locations do not reduce that much during recession periods even though the cost of purchasing such a unit does.

3. Cash is King

Remember that cash is King! Use your strong negotiating position with and influx of cash to gain bargains. Do not be afraid to shop around and to wait. Work at your own pace, do your research, and do not be rushed into making a decision by others. If you have a pile of cash, you call the shots!

4. Think Twice Before Setting Up or Buying Businesses

Don't be too quick to set up or buy into businesses. Business Fundamentals are important at this point because opportunities that looked good during a boom period might not be so great during a recession.

With cash flow being tight and spending reduced, businesses that are recession proof will be hard to come by, luxury products and goods will be non-priorities during this period, as will goods that are not deemed as necessities.

When making decisions at this time a very important question to ask is *"Will people still buy this product or use this service during this recession period, when everyone is cutting down expenses?"*

If you are looking at setting up companies, you cannot do so with a mindset that the economy will turn around, but whether the venture can be profitable in the current economic climate. You must be realistic with the possibility that you might have to weather the storm for a long period of time and make decisions accordingly.

5. Engage in Strategic People Partnerships

Look for people partnerships that can bring you greater returns for your investment. There might be good people during this period of recession with good work ethic and excellent character who might be struggling with the wrong type of job or business which does not suit their skill sets. So at this time, when you have an influx of cash, you can either get these people who need a change and are looking for work to work for you, or set up small businesses with them. Their skills, energy and work ethic can be a great asset to you to capitalize on recession proof opportunities.

6. Transition Into Recession Proof Industries

You need to transition into jobs and business that can survive or thrive in a recession. Not every job or business will thrive in a recession. Some will find that their vocations in certain industries will be terminated.

Which jobs and vocations are still needed in both good and bad times? Are policemen less needed in a bad time? Are governments quick to lay off staff during a recession? These are some pertinent questions you must ask and do research on. Each country's economic environment is different, and certain types of jobs or business deemed recession proof in one country may not be at all in another.

You must transition from jobs where there is more supply than demand or ones that will phase out during a recession. You also might need to restructure your business before the recession, or diversify to a more cash intensive model so that you can get regular cash flow during a recession.

Understand the times and make wise decisions accordingly.

7. Plan Towards Self-Reliance of Basic Needs

You must start putting plans into place to own your own food supply and shelter before a recession comes. During a major recession or depression, food will become extremely expensive, huge conglomerates are already working towards controlling the price of food and farms so that they can dictate prices and control the global economy as to the prices of goods. The same thing that happened with Diamonds and De Beers will also happen with basic food items.

As an organization or individual, you must take steps to own your own food supply. Learn about Urban Farming and community lots where you as a neighborhood can grow your own supply. There are already clubs and associations working towards this and you can join the right ones. Don't join those that only preach doom and gloom without intelligence and basis, but moderate groups that are concerned about healthy organic food and food supply.

8. Avoid Any Unnecessary Upgrading Expenditure

Don't upscale your house or car or any other unneeded expenditure before a recession. Even if times look good and you feel you can afford it, do not make large purchases with cash or on credit just before a recession. You need to read the signals and understand what is happening. If you are living an adequate, and not an extravagant lifestyle, you must maintain this at all costs. If your lifestyle is extravagant (I deem extravagance as spending your whole income every month) without much savings then you will need to change and downscale your lifestyle, before a recession fully hits. It is also very important to have a basic home, not an extravagant one.

"Understand the times and make wise decisions accordingly."

Good homes in good locations price themselves highly. Boom times might be good times to unload properties that you will not be able to sustain (because it is on high credit) during a recession. If you bought a property for investment purposes it is important to cash in on the investment while you still can before prices drop.

Maintain a reasonable home with basic features that you need. My mentor, Dr Jonathan David, has lived in the same house for more than 25 years even though he has the means to upgrade his house and lifestyle significantly. If you are already struggling to maintain a home because it is opulent and expensive then you are going to struggle even more during the recession.

What You Can Do During a Depression

1. Weather Volatility By Owning Your Food Supply

Prepare for the volatility of currency depreciation by owning your own food supply. In a depression the price of basic items such as food and other necessities might increase dramatically because of sudden depreciation of currency. It might be a great idea to be prepared by owning your own food supply. Grow your own vegetables if you have a garden, and raise fish, as it takes up very little space to do so. This will dramatically reduce your food bill and make you less affected by dramatic increases in food costs.

Owning a small farm, or pooling your resources with others to own your own farm, will be a great way to protect your family and others close to you and ensure consistent food supply.

2. Keep Ready Cash At Hand

Keep some of your resources in ready cash that is easily accessible. During a depression there have been runs on banks, meaning everybody flocks to the banks to withdraw their money. If you are one of the later ones trying to do this, you need to be aware that banks can run out of ready cash as they don't keep the exact amount of money you've deposited. This is due to banks' fractional reserve lending system and heavy involvement in electronic transactions.

You need to keep some cash readily accessible to you and your family in a safe and secure location close to you. A home safe or a safety deposit box in a secure location are good ideas to think about. Your cash must be close by and in an accessible place as you may need to get to in case of an emergency.

3. Hedge Against Currency Devaluation With Some Precious Metals

Hedge your cash against currency devaluation by converting some to precious metals such as gold or silver.

There is often a lack of consumer confidence during a recession and this can also affect the value of currency. Most currency today, including the U.S. Dollar is no longer backed by gold. In the past, to print money, countries had to have the required store of gold deposits to back the currency. This is no longer the case with many countries relying on goodwill and public and business perception of their currency, and because of this currency depreciation is a real threat.

In a depression scenario it would pay to keep a portion of your resources in gold and silver. When I say this I mean actual physical gold and silver, not paper ownership as some organizations are trying to sell you.

4. Position Yourself in Industries that Have Relevance

Work at business and jobs that have relevance during the depression period. One of the areas that you are going to be hit is built income, but those with income are going to have opportunities to capitalize on land and other resources cheaply because people are going to need cash. The key is to be in jobs and businesses that are relevant to the times.

For example, owning a farm producing food is still going to be relevant; owning a luxury restaurant might not be. Businesses that provide basic necessities such as basic level education for children, public transport, food supply, and basic housing are still going to be necessities even in a recession.

5. Invest Into Strategic Alliances Before the Depression

Use your money and skills to build strategic relationships that can be of mutual help you both during the depression. Sowing your skills, time, and resources accurately during good times will build strategic relationships that you can connect with and make use of during any economic climate. Some businesses and government bodies still need to spend to empower communities and on education and other products and services even during the worst of times. While these spending, even those relevant to your business may be cut down, there will still need to be some spending and these will go to people who are trusted and known.

If you make strategic connections during the worst of times you will be able to network with these connections, so build trust that can become valuable to you even during a depression period. You will have customers who will lead you to opportunities and get you connected to businesses and jobs during the worst of times as well. Choose your strategic contacts wisely, they must have permanence and a great reputation that has been maintained over years.

6. Be Part of a Community of Like-Minded Individuals

Get involved in organizations with similar and accurate mindsets so you have a community to rely on during a depression. Being a loner with individual strength during a depression is one of the worst things you can do. People are social beings so you must have organizations and relationships that you can count on. Church groups, associations, religious organizations with accurate mindsets are communities that you can count on during the worst of times.

Villages in the old days used to rely on each other as a community to survive bad periods. We need to go back to this way of living and to get our neighborhoods to be more proactive at the very least. If you are unable to connect with the neighborhood where you live, find one that you can connect with outside. Choose wisely. What you are looking for is an organization or an association with strong community ties and accurate leadership to get the whole body of people through this difficult period.

7. Keep Buoyant and Sharp in Spirit and Mind

Keep your spirit buoyant and your mind sharp during this short period. Depressions normally range from a three to four year period; it will not go on forever. It is just an economic period to get through, as such you should not allow yourself or your children to go through this period with fear. Also do not even anticipate this period in fear.

If you have done proper financial planning and management during the boom and recession times you will survive the depression. The key is that the principles taught throughout this book are strictly adhered to. Follow the principles and concepts given from Chapter One, right through to the last chapter and implement them in your life to stay on course.

Keep your spirit buoyant by always visualizing the possibilities that can happen to you even during a depression. Our God is not contained by any economic condition, and you can be blessed and thrive in any environment and in any economic condition.

Find people you can connect with and talk to when things are tough. You must have your tribe of mutual support. Just knowing that you have people ready to help and that you are not alone on this journey can keep you extremely buoyant.

8. Be Set Up for Trade Before the Depression

You must set yourself up for trade before a depression hits. Find out what others want during a depression and set yourself up to be the answer.

Is it to have jobs? Is it to open up new markets or food supply? It is possible to survive and thrive during a recession, however, the key is to be the answer. What are people going to be desperate for? I think certainly not more cars or luxury homes. It will be the basic everyday items that they are going to need to survive, and that includes an income as well.

You also have to think about what will hold value during a recession and depression and get rid of unwanted investments you are going to be burdened with. Make investments into businesses, farms, basic items that people are going to need before a recession comes.

In Summary

An economic boom, recession, and depression are just economic processes that countries go through. You can weather the storm with accurate preparations just like anything in life, and what is more is when you know when it is coming through reading the signs, so your preparation gives you an edge over those who are not prepared.

Central to these preparations are the concepts and tools given in this book. You and your children must build the right financial practices and habits from the start. The discipline and diligence during the good times is what will set you up to survive and thrive during the bad periods.

Below are some tips that I have learned from my mentor, Dr. Jonathan David, who teaches on the topic extensively. I have adapted them for this chapter.

- Save 20% of your income in anticipation of lean times during a recession.

- Live a lifestyle of adequacy, not extravagance during times of good economic growth. This is so you can save easier and have access to funds during a recession.

- You need to conserve by downsizing, conserving and consolidating when moving into lean years and those of a recession. Continuous gearing (high loans) with no end to keep the business growing will only lead to more pressure and stress during periods where we are not operating in the same abundance.

- Collectibles and Antiques will lose their value and importance during a recession. These are items that operate in a fickle environment.

- Have some of your money in precious metals such as gold and silver; it can be a hedge against the devaluation of currency.

- Devise action steps to pay off unprofitable borrowings and debts quickly.

- Save and multiply investments for your children's education.

- Have adequate insurance protection for medical emergencies. I personally know of families that have been wiped out during a recession because a close family member fell into a medical emergency. It is better you to invest in medical coverage for your parents or the aged to protect them against any unforeseen incident than to be caught with a huge medical bill yourself.

- We must be good stewards of all that is given to us and we cannot rely on others to manage our money for us. I personally believe managing our money is everyone's first business.

- Learn to take advantage of taxation benefits, credit and good debt to allow us breathing space, but do not over commit to what you can afford to pay back. A good guide is that you must be able to pay back loans you take even in a recession. If you think your business is going to contract during that period, or that you might be out of a job, then you cannot afford to make that investment. It sounds great to say I have bought five properties, but they are not yours until you have fully paid for them.

Dr. Jonathan David has written many other good materials on the topic and you can source them from his website www.drjonathan-david.org.

**EXERCISE: Working the Economic Cycles
Money Management in a Recession**

For Ages 5-10

Cut their pocket money in half for a week, and teach them skills to survive this period. Show them at the end of the exercise that they might go through a time where they don't have the same amount of money as they are used to and they need to save for that period. Ask them what a good amount to save is? Work them towards 20%.

Ask them to imagine that they were an adult and get them to tell you what difficulties they could imagine they might go through, or even what you could face as a parent. If they have difficulty, prompt them with some questions and give them suggestions to get the process moving.

For Ages 11-17

Give them homework and Google various economic catastrophes such as the great depression, the recent Greek incident, and even the US sub-prime crisis. Teach them and show them what has happened to people who are not prepared for those times. Also teach them what happened to those with excess cash who liquidated their investments before the crash happened. Talk to them about recessions, boom times and depressions as explained in this book, and get them to draw up a plan to survive each part. Get them to imagine they are running their own business.

These exercises and research projects could take four weeks, one for each economic period.

Chapter 10

Winning at Business Early
Training a Successful Entrepreneur Under
Your Roof

As a child develops, grows, watches and learns from observing parents, they begin to pick up capabilities that can be used in their first business. Both my wife and I run our own companies. I run a multinational training company with a business partner and my wife runs a copywriting and translation company from home.

This was planned. My wife was a good lawyer and was offered a junior partnership in the firm where she was working and had a bright future in the legal industry. We both felt, however, that one of us should work from home and run a part time business so that our children could watch and observe a business environment and learn to become independent with entrepreneurial skills that they could use in any field.

My daughter was two and a half years old when she started mimicking her mother selling to clients. She would pretend to pick up the phone and tele-market to 'potential' clients! She even mimicked the sales pitch, even though she could not yet pronounce some words correctly. At two and a half years of age she sat in at strategy meetings where we discussed how to grow the business.

Today she is six years old and has her first business which she started when she was five and a half years old. Her business is making greeting cards by hand (with the supervision of her mother) and then selling them. She identifies prospects, makes the sales pitch and convinces them to buy the cards. It has also been good for her to learn to handle rejection when they don't buy, because she is learning how to overcome disappointment and continue trying again.

She has had to learn profit and loss and to support the cause that she has identified. 50% of what she earns is given to our church for its building fund. She tithes 10% and the remaining 40% is used to buy a toy, a book, or similar item that she would like (which is identified at the onset). When she achieves the amount needed to buy the toy (from the 40% of profits allocated), she gets to go and purchase that item.

I spent some time explaining this because I want you to understand some key outcomes that have happened after my daughter started her business. Some obvious benefits, as one would call them, include he following:

- My daughter's confidence has improved
- Her math ability has increased
- She understands concepts such as profit and loss
- She understands money for a purpose, and feels pride to support a worthy cause, and she now wants to give some of the business money to provide proper meals for orphans, for an orphanage she visited
- She has the ability to communicate with adults and to explain herself
- She has no fear of public speaking

There are even more benefits than these that will stay with her throughout her entire life, and this is the reason why we chose to model entrepreneurship. Imagine if it is your child, and imagine that this child has already grown older under this type of training. Just think about the possibilities!

Benefits of Developing the Mind of an Entrepreneur in Your Child

Here are some ways your child will benefit from learning the skills and mindset of entrepreneurship at an early age:

1. They are Able to Resource Themselves

Children with the mind of an entrepreneur and the skills to match are able to resource themselves for whatever purpose they may choose.

Whether your child wants to take up a social cause, work as an academic, or run a business, entrepreneurial skills will put a spirit in your child to be able to resource themselves to achieve any goal. I am not just talking about financial resources but mental strength, fortitude, tenacity and the necessary skills for success in life. They will become self-sufficient in every area they need to be.

2. They Will Become Boundary Breakers

The entrepreneurial spirit is the spirit and ability to break new boundaries that people have never broken before, to invent new things and break barriers. It is the spirit of doing what everybody else says is impossible. Successful entrepreneurs achieve what others say cannot be done in fields that are extremely competitive. This skill allows children to break boundaries in sports, their studies, with social levels, music and in any field they operate in. They will not be limited by what people say about their chosen field.

3. They Become Highly Innovative

Innovation is a hallmark of successful entrepreneurs. The entrepreneurial mindset and spirit is a highly innovative one that exemplifies creativity, ingenuity and the ability to build new things, and to pioneer what has never been done before to creatively engineer the future of humanity.

4. They are Resilient

True entrepreneurs have a spirit of being able to weather any storm and stay resilient in the most adverse of circumstances. They have an ability to rise in difficult times when everyone else around them would be struggling in the same situation.

Other Key Benefits

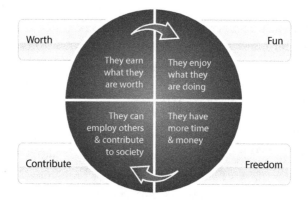

Modeling – Using Your Occupation to Teach Business

Most children are very interested in what their parents do. There is an immediate affinity and affection as well as an excitement when they are younger. Don't be afraid of talking about your work or business with your children. Everything that everyone does is important. Good work is something to be proud of. Work is something that provides for us and if we are people who have found our passion at work, we are immediately people who are blessed.

The best way for you to teach your children all of the above is for you to model being an entrepreneur and living this kind of lifestyle. If you want your children to be resilient, they have to see you living it and understand that resilience is a way of life. If they see that you have no problem resourcing yourself to buy that property or invest in their future, then they will live the same way. You cannot teach what you don't live. I strongly encourage you to start something, even if it is part time.

In the old days parents used to send children (as a compulsory extra-curricular activity) to learn music as they felt it was a skill their children needed in life. Today, the skills our children are going to need more than ever are entrepreneurial and financial management skills. Start building it into them by you simply starting to do something yourself.

If you have a full time job, here are some ideas of things you can do where you can involve your children as well, if they are older:

- Sell something you are both passionate about at a flea market
- Join a Multi-level company that does not force you to pay too much for stock, or to take up too many unnecessary products and whose philosophy you believe in
- Meet customers and do something part-time like selling insurance or unit trusts
- Write a book
- Write music and produce an album
- Make a short documentary
- Start your own online business

- Offer writing or translation services, something part time
- Develop a mobile app
- Build a portal to sell second hand goods
- Start a food kiosk

You also have to talk to your children about your occupation to get them excited about what you are doing. If you can take them to your work place and show them what you are doing, that is even better.

Start young. Involve them in what you are doing by sharing with them and building their capability before it is too late.

This is how you can do that:

- Tell them about your occupation
- Talk to them about strategy and how you think your company could be better, sell better, work better (don't complain about the management but be constructive)
- Explain the process of how your product is developed, where it originates from, and why people buy it
- Explain who buys it, and how it is sold
- Explain what is unique about it, and how it overcomes other competitors
- Every day, tell them something positive that happened at work
- If there is something bad that has happened, let's say, you need to shut down your business or you lost your job, talk to them about it and tell them you are going to try something else (they will remember how resilient you were about your business, and it can be a powerful lesson for them)

What Age Is the Right Age?

As our company has already trained close to 10, 000 entrepreneurs in various businesses, each of them achieving an average increase in income of between 100 to 400 percent within one month, we are known as experts in the field of entrepreneur development.

I've always had a plan, however, to teach my own children to become entrepreneurs by the time they were five or six years old and to teach this to others around the world. I wanted to give parents an opportunity to give their children the freedom to resource themselves by doing what they are passionate about.

I think a good age to start is at the age of five years old. At this age their brain has developed enough to understand concepts and the world around them. They also need to understand people and how to connect with them. This is why I suggest this age. You can start younger if you want and feel that your child is ready.

It can be more of a play project with serious overtones. The key when starting with children at a young age is to motivate them and to keep it fun. The more fun they have, the more it creates a good experience which forms and reinforces a mindset that business is fun and easy (which it is) and they will not hesitate to try this when they are older.

However, if your child is already older, don't worry because you can start whatever the age of your child. If they start older, they can do more and learn quicker, so they will not miss out. There is no competition here, so enjoy the process with your children and let them enjoy it as well. This is the only rule. Follow the principles in this book as well to ensure success.

The Best Way to Teach Your Children

It's important not to push your children too fast, but also don't be too slow with them either. In fact, I think age has very little to do with it. Of course there are things that will be too difficult for a five-year-old to grasp (like high school grade *Advance Mathematics*), but you will be surprised what you can teach your children if you follow these simple concepts of teaching:

1. Break Concepts Down Into Bite Sizes

Break concepts down into simple and manageable bite sizes to teach a whole concept.

We have been able to teach business concepts and investment concepts that even most adults have difficulty understanding to illiterate and poor communities because we know how to break them down into smaller bits of information that enables anyone to learn. One parent asked me, when they looked at our syllabus for teaching children finance, whether it was really possible to teach children these concepts as even he had difficulty understanding them. Well, when we actually taught it to his son, he realized that information is often simpler when you break it down into bite sizes.

2. Stimulate a Desire for Learning in Your Child

Stimulate your child when you are teaching by making it fun and enjoyable for them so they want to learn.

I made math fun for my daughter Mia. The more she thought that math was fun and like riddles, the more she wanted to do more and more of them. She could do additions and subtractions up to a million or more without knowing how to pronounce and read a million in numbers. You can push the boundaries of what children can learn if you keep this simple rule. Make it fun and engage them.

3. Make the Complex Simple and Don't Project How Smart You Are

I don't know how many teachers and trainers seem to forget the basics. Someone who is teaching needs to make the complex simple and not make it more complicated to make more money or to show people how good they are.

One of the best ways to assess your teaching or training ability is to gauge how much of what you are teaching is actually implemented and understood, not how much people are impressed with you.

4. Praise and Reward their Understanding and Implementation

Give them rewards when they understand what you teach and praise them when they implement it.

All children love praise from their parents and while you can challenge them to do better, you must never forget to keep praising them and encouraging them. When they achieve certain milestones like selling their first product, make sure you celebrate it. When they use what you taught them and applied it, like calculating cost for the first time, be as excited as they are. Remember they are smaller than you, and younger than you, but by encouraging them and rewarding implementation of behaviors, they will want to do better and will continue being excited by this business.

5. Build, Model, and Teach Excellence

Build, model, and teach excellence to train them with the understanding that their business can succeed as much as they can grow.

You can begin to build excellence in your child by modeling it yourself. Children pick up what they observe. Excellence is also a spirit and this spirit, if you have it, can be transferred to your children. Excellence is giving your best and doing things to your best level or even better than that, if possible, with every opportunity that is given to you. People who live by this attitude of excellence succeed in life.

Always challenge your children when they do shoddy work and encourage them to be better by giving their best. Tell them people are paying their hard earned money for your product and you need to give them the best, not just sell to make money.

Encourage them to sell to the best of their ability, plan and work to their best as well this will begin to build a habit of excellence in them.

Always remember though, that it will all fail if you as a parent fail to model it.

What They Can Do At Different Age Levels

While I believe that there are no limitations to what any child can do, some parents need some guidelines, so I have given you some suggestions here. (These are not definitive or exhaustive).

Age Group	Types of Business
5 - 8 year olds	Arts and Craft type of business, reselling or trading goods like bracelets, beads designs, earings etc. Make Cards, Make colourful hand paintings and sell them
9 - 12 Year olds	Food businesses, selling snacks, arts and craft businesses with more complex designs and materials, trading goods and supplies. Write a simple story book. Sell paintings.
15 - 20 Year olds	App Development, Websites, Portal an other e commerce businesses using social media and other forms of internet and e-commerce based solutions, write a book, do something with passive income, Work an MLM business with products their peers need. They Can carve wood, do sculptures or pottery and sell it, paint or make a music album with their friends. Let them explore anything that can make money
21 - 27 year olds	ANYTHING THEY WANT! They are talented enough to do it

Characteristics of Breakthrough Entrepreneurs

These are the characteristics of breakthrough entrepreneurs and this is what you need to train your child up in:

1. They Have Drive

Drive is something entrepreneurs must have if they want to overcome obstacles. It helps them break limitations that would

kill other people. It helps them focus and achieve goals no matter how others are working. Drive is internal. It is an energy that
can be harnessed through passion and thinking of benefiting
others around you.

2. They Have Integrity

Business without integrity is a waste of time. What is the
point of breaking rules, bribing and stealing to get your way
to the top only to have yourself arrested and thrown in jail?
Work with integrity. Success at all costs is greed, and greed
is never good and will eventually land you in jail. Integrity
attracts success and other good people to work with you. Dis-
honesty attracts trouble and other crooks to work with you.
You decide what you want for your life and family.

3. They Have the Ability to Troubleshoot

They have the ability to work out problems and find cre-
ative solutions when others can't.

There are two types of people that apply for a job with us.
One sees problems and needs us to tell them what to do, while
the other sees problems and tries to come up with a solution,
and they sometimes implement a solution without even telling us. Which one do you think succeeds with us? Which one
do you think succeeds in life? I have a rule at work, which is if
you come to me with a problem you must give me a solution.
It does not have to be the right solution, but a solution that
you have come up with to the best of your ability.

4. They are Solution Oriented

They are solution oriented and know that every solution
has a problem. They look for and use problems as stepping-
stones to move up higher, from one solution to the next.

Some people, however, see problems as roadblocks, others see solutions as opportunities to capitalize and move up
higher, where still others just see problems. Your child needs

to have a worldview of possibilities. When they can catch the spirit of possibility and that it is possible to overcome every problem, they will achieve more than others can. Always share with them your perspective of possibilities and how you view the world and its problems and limitations (Provided your worldview is one of possibilities and is accurate).

5. They Know How to Synergize With People

My mentor continually told me that success is not a solo project. Successful entrepreneurs know how to synergize with people and how to bring the potential that they have to win with them. Successful businesses have synergy; different people with different strengths equalizing the company to win.

6. They are Excellent Communicators

Entrepreneurs who are successful know how to communicate and win with people. A staff member I had to correct on certain issues, once told me that she felt that every time after I had spoken to her about her mistakes, she would leave my office feeling more confident and better about herself. This motivated her to keep changing and to become better at her job.

It is important to talk and communicate with people to drive them to reach their potential. If you do, even when you are correcting them, they will appreciate you. Find the right words and plan what you want to say, there are no short cuts.

7. They are Able to Connect With Anyone

Connection skills are very important core skill that we teach entrepreneurs. Good entrepreneurs know how to connect at different levels, from a CEO of a big multinational to a security guard at the entrance of that multinational. The key is not to make others think that you are great, but make others feel great when they are with you.

8. They Challenge the Accepted Norms of the Status Quo

They push the boundaries of what is accepted and what is the normal and standard for the industry.

When I first started my business, and started to build the cause of getting people out of poverty by teaching them how to start their own business, many people would tell me it couldn't be done. I also had many people telling me that it was impossible for an Asian company to have a multinational presence in western countries without pumping in huge amounts of money. I learnt an important lesson when I was twenty-one and started my first business; Successful entrepreneurs push the boundaries of what is accepted and what is the 'normal' outcome. In fact, they capitalize on what has never been done before.

9. They Are Highly Innovative

They are highly innovative and continue to stay innovative and at a cutting edge to remain relevant.

Innovation for making things better, improving yourself, and doing things that nobody else is doing, are what can keep an entrepreneur highly successful. It's great to become successful, but it's more important to stay successful. If you are an entrepreneur who is not innovative, you either have to change fast or gather innovative people around you to compensate for your lack. No business stays static and thrives in the long-run.

10. They Live for a Cause, Not Money

A cause is what drives you to success, not driving for more money. If you live a worthy cause and are passionate about it, you attract people to you. If your life, walk and talk are all about making more money for yourself, people will run. As an entrepreneur you need people to like you and to like your business.

I once had a high-level bank director say to me, *"I must make sure our bank works with you to support your cause. I am going to talk to the CEO about you, and all our directors, because they need to know about you and what you are doing, and our bank needs to be part of it".*

That person did just that and we are now working with this major bank. A cause can galvanize your business and take it to the next level faster than anything else can.

Group Versus Individual Start-Ups

Should you let your children work in a group (if they are thirteen years and above) or as an individual? I have worked with young children in both scenarios.

When children work at business as a group, they will need to have a motivated adult who is going to spend time developing and mentoring them. The chosen adult cannot be overbearing. Different children will be at different levels, therefore, the adult will need to be patient with the children and discover the grace and giftings of each one to equalize the group.

The key to success, regardless of working as a group or as an individual, is that there must be deadlines, targets, and research goals clearly defined.

A Lesson Plan for Children of Different Age Groups

The way this table works is an ascending table of learning from left to right according to age, which means that ages five through to eight will learn those topics and stop there. In contrast, children between the ages of nine to thirteen will learn the topics that the five to eight year olds are learning but in a bit more complex way in addition to what they are learning for their specific age group. Ages thirteen through to seventeen have to study, and do some Googling or research on all the topics. This is so that they can have an in-depth knowledge on al the topics the other age groups (aged five through seventeen) have to learn.

Topic	Ages 5 - 8	Ages 9 - 13	Ages 13 - 19
Sales	How to come up with a pitch and sell their product	Understand the best ways to sell their product (Sales strategy)	Understand what are their best strategy for the business they like is
Best Practices	What is the best way to sell & to who to sell to	How are people doing this and becoming successful what are best practices	Understand what are their best strategy for the business they like is
Math	Basic Profit, Loss, to calculate what they can do about their business	Learn about higher level math to calculate profit and loss and about tax, savings and investment	Learn basic accounting, tax calculations and how to keep cost and overheads low
Profit and Loss	Teach them basic cost and what are the components of the cost and that they can use only the profit margin. Teach them basics of profit and loss	Talk to you child about how they can increase profit and minimize cost, and explain how others do it in business. Work a plan with them	Ask Your child to develop strategies or learn strategies to maximize profit. Learn case studies of businesses relevant to their field and work through how to implement it in their own business. Study implementable cutting edge business books together
Quality and Standards	Talk to them about value and that their products must have value to sell. And how they must do things well and to their best every time	Get them to understand value sells, and ask them to plan how they can add value to their business. Show them other successful business and teach them how value and quality standards has helped those businesses	How can they create systematic value for their customers and how they can raise the quality and standards, without raising the cost too much in their business. Teach them quality vs price. What is acceptable quality of a product and why they always need to be higher than the acceptable standards, but not too high to make the product uncompetitive because people don't what to pay for that sort of quality
Innovation	Teach them what innovation is, and ask them to make their product slightly unique	Give them case studies of innovative companies, Air Asia, Apple and Samsung and teach them how they innovate to lead in their business	Read the Book Blue Ocean Strategies by W. Chan Kim and Renée Mauborgne and implement the concepts into your childs business
Integrity	How to be honest with your money and your product	Giving good value for money, serving the customer	What are principles of business integrity, how to treat employees, why bribing is wrong

You can keep adding topics and customizing this to suit your development plan with your own children.

Some Useful Tools for Coaching Your Children

These are weekly mentoring tools that you can use with older children to create momentum for their business. Only share the tools with older children who can understand and use it, for them to work and plan with. Basically, our aim is to involve them in the process.

Week 1

The week one tool should be used to plan the overall structure of what you should be doing for the rest of the weeks to come. You can add or change this structure to suit your needs, as it is just a guideline.

Week 2-4 and Beyond

The week 2- 4 plan allows you to systematically work through the plan you have set and keep it on track every week. You must work according to the capabilities and interest level of the child. Most children love business, however, don't drive them until they start hating it. That would be the worst possible outcome!

Gap Areas

Gap areas are areas in the child's business that need to improve to give more value to customers. It could be product quality, lack of a sales plan, lack of skills, or lack of innovation. Identify the gaps and work through them week by week to close that gap by training your child on these capabilities and competencies. This improves their business as well as your child's capability and capacity for life in the process.

Week 1 Planning Sheet

Part of the three steps for each child must be something

that involves selling their product to people. While they can also do research, one of the steps must be going out there and promoting or selling the product. If this is not done they will not grow and learn as fast as others.

Week 2-4 Mentoring Structure

What we want is for the children to take three steps to grow their business to the next level every week. They must start selling from week one immediately.

Week 1 Planning Sheet

WEEKLY AGENDA	Time Per Topic	Gap Areas Week 1	Research – Mentor
Week 1			1.
1.			2.
2.			3.
3.			4.
Week 2			5.
1.			6.
2.			7.
3.		Role Play Planned	Research – Mentor
4.			1.
Week 3			2.
1.			3.
2.			4.
3.		3 Steps Wk 1	Personal or Group Learning Visit
4.		1.	
Week 4		2.	
1.		3.	
2.		Notes And Remarks	
3.			
4.			

Week 2-4 Mentoring Structure

Agenda	Time	Last Weeks Research	
1.		1.	
		2.	
2.		3.	
		4.	
3.		5.	
		6.	
Gap Areas to be discussed		Next weeks Research Mentee	Research – Mentor
1.		1.	
		2.	
2.		3.	
		4.	
3.		5.	Personal / Group Learning Visit
		6.	

Time To work on Gap & Research > Date and Time During the Week						

Notes and Remarks	3 Steps Wk 2	
	1.	
	2.	
	3.	

Profiling Your Child

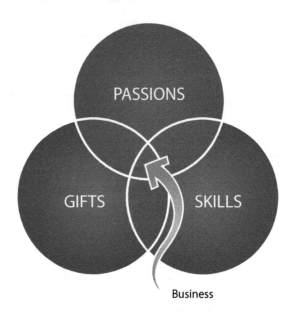

Business

Profile your children by identifying what their gifts, skills, and passions are. People always succeed at what they are passionate about as well as what they are gifted for. For example, if your child has an artistic gift or a musical one, and that's what they are passionate about, then that should be what they start to do. Don't worry so much about skills, you can help them develop them along the way.

The more entrepreneurs we train, the more we realize that passions actually drive everything else. If you are passionate, you will keep practicing, and develop skills and talent. Some children are naturally talented at certain things.

They need to either develop a product with you or trade a product they buy. For example, in my daughter's case we knew she had passion for artistic pursuits, so we decided to talk to her about making cards and also selling small rubber toys that worked as erasers, but we let her decide. It's okay if your child decides on something but then changes their mind and wants to try something else later. The important thing is that they are actually trying and doing something.

Once you have identified the business idea, the following are the skills you need to discover and teach them:

- Sales skills – how to sell and prepare a sales pitch.

- How are you going to sell – meeting people face to face or through the phone? Via the Internet?

- Sales Strategy (for older children) – What is the best way to get the product to the customers? How to make it exciting for them and to make a reasonable profit while keeping cost down.

- Innovation – What can I do with my product that will give it an edge over competitors?

- Delivery and quality – how can I ensure consistent quality and delivery of my product?

- What would be the potential problems with this business and how will I resolve them?

- Profit and loss- how do I increase my profits and keep my cost down?

- Partnering with others (for older children) – How do I identify the grace of others and work with them to increase competitiveness of my business?

- Get them to develop a business card and a website (for older children) There are websites online where you can download or design your website in templates before uploading it. These websites teach you everything you need to do develop a simple e-commerce platform.

- Teach them how to use Facebook to do their business, (there are many online guides how to do this.)

Develop a plan to teach them each topic week by week, but get them to start selling or developing a product straight away as they keep working on the business. Who knows they might be the next IT billionaire or might make a couple of thousand dollars? The amount does not matter. What does matter is that they try and become entrepreneurs.

If they do become successful as a young entrepreneur from what you have taught them from this book, write to me and let me know. I don't want their money, but would want to use their story to inspire others.

EXERCISE: Winning At Business Early
Training a Successful Entrepreneur under
your Roof

For Ages 5-12

1. Profile your children to find out what their natural talents and passions are and then get them to start a business along those lines.

2. Teach them profit and loss with their business and cost as well.

3. Ask them to identify their cause and who they will give 50% of their profits to as charity to that cause.

4. Ask them to identify their source that they want to give a tithe of 10% to

5. Get them to identify something exciting to do for themselves with their 40% profit. This is what will motivate them. If necessary take them to a toy shop.

6. Don't set a target that's too high, make it a reasonable amount for a reasonable toy (if it's too expensive and this exercise takes too long it will discourage them and not work).

7. Get them to start and encourage them every step of the way and guide them where you need to. They need to work at it and talk to people and sell their products - don't do it for them. If they need support stand with them or behind them when they are doing it.

8. If they fall short of the target, explain this to them, and top up the amount so that they can get the toy, but be sure to tell them next time they will need to achieve it on their own.

9. Repeat the process after a short break to give them and yourself some rest.

For Ages 13-17

1. Identify their skills, gifts and passions.

2. Ask them to identify an area they are passionate about

3. Ask them to pick a business that they can start.

4. Try to ensure (but this is not compulsory) that the business can be promoted on Facebook, and online, as well as via face-to-face selling.

5. Help them identify their cause and whom they will give 50% of the profits to.

6. Help them identify the source they want to tithe 10% of their profits to.

7. Help them work through what they should do with the 40%. It could be to start their next business, pay for a car when they are in college or even contribute towards their own education.

8. A portion of it must be used for investment and building wealth according to the principles in this book.

9. Let them explore, develop, and work through the business, or shut it down if they want to and feel it's not working to try other things.

10. Tell them to grow it and keep it going even when they enter university. They might need a business income and have capability to develop it there instead of just getting a job like everyone else.

Invitation to Write

Thank you for taking the time to read this book. It is my sincerest hope that this book has been of value and service to you.

As I have mentioned in the last chapter, if your children (or even yourself) have become successful as a result of what you have learned from this book, please write to me and let me know. I would really like to use their story to inspire others.

Or, if you have been helped, inspired, or touched by this book in any way shape or form, and feel you want to share your story, please write to me about it as well.

What challenges do you face? What battles have you won? How have you been helped or perhaps how were you empowered to help someone else?

I would love to read about your journey in developing your Money Quotient and building your wealth.

Sincere Regards,
Raymond Gabriel

Write to me at:
Email:
moneyquotient@raymondgabriel.com

Snail Mail:
No 4 Jalan SS 22/10
Damansara Jaya, 47400 Petaling Jaya,Selangor,Malaysia

Connect Online:
Website:
www.raymondgabriel.com

Facebook:
www.facebook.com/RaymondGabrielAuthor

CPSIA information can be obtained
at www.ICGtesting.com
Printed in the USA
FSHW012101210419
57463FS

9 789671 340806